THE ROYAL LIFE SAVING SOCIETY
UNITED KINGDOM

Life Saving
and
Water Safety

PRICE 5/- *plus postage*

Published by

THE ROYAL LIFE SAVING SOCIETY
United Kingdom

Headquarters:
Desborough House, 14 Devonshire St., Portland Place, London WIN 2AT
Telephone: 01 580-5678/5679   Telegrams: Natatorium London

1st EDITION, 1963
2nd EDITION, 1969

Printed in Great Britain by Spottiswoode, Ballantyne & Co. Ltd.
London and Colchester

THE ROYAL LIFE SAVING SOCIETY

Founded 1891   Incorporated by Royal Charter

Patron:
HER MAJESTY THE QUEEN

Grand President:
ADMIRAL OF THE FLEET
THE EARL MOUNTBATTEN OF BURMA
K.G., P.C., G.C.B., O.M., G.C.S.I., G.C.I.E., G.C.V.O., D.S.O., F.R.S.

UNITED KINGDOM

President:
SIR HENRY STUDDY, C.B.E.

Deputy President:
S. E. PECK, ESQ., B.E.M., D.L.

Prepared by the National Technical Committee

Chairman: F. Fenn

Members: Miss A. L. Fettes, G. C. Andrews, T. Baptie, K. R. Bennetto, D. Cheetham, J. Curtis, B.E.M., E. C. Sherwood, J. Stebbing, A. G. Thompson, J. C. Wheeler.

Medical Advisers: Dr. E. K. Gardner, M.B., F.R.C.S., F.F.A.R.C.S. Dr. P. Drummond, M.B., B.S., D.I.H.

The Committee acknowledge with gratitude the work of many others in comment and advice.

Foreword

For over 75 years the Royal Life Saving Society has carried out its voluntary work in the cause of reducing loss of life from drowning. Today the Society is firmly established Commonwealth wide. In Canada, Australia and New Zealand there are large National Branches, who have their own handbooks and whose new ideas and techniques have been most useful in the preparation of this new edition of the United Kingdom National Branch Handbook, which will itself provide the basis of instruction in many other countries of the Commonwealth.

Our object, of course, is to save life, but in mastering the technique there is a physical and mental challenge which will be found to provide a splendid and worthwhile form of recreation for people of all ages, particularly the young. This challenge also helps to draw together the peoples of the Commonwealth in a common humanitarian purpose. Throughout the Commonwealth the Society awards more than a third of a million proficiency awards every year.

As Grand President, I take this opportunity of wishing all those who serve the Society and its cause all success in their excellent work.

Mountbatten of Burma
A.F.

Grand President

Table of

Contents

THE AIMS OF THE SOCIETY
As laid down in the 1924 Charter:

(a) To promote technical education in life saving and the resuscitation of the apparently drowned;

(b) to stimulate public opinion in favour of the general adoption of swimming and life saving as a branch of instruction in schools, colleges, etc.;

(c) to encourage floating, diving, plunging and such other swimming arts as would be of assistance to a person endeavouring to save life;

(d) to arrange and promote public lectures, demonstrations and competitions, and to form classes of instruction, so as to bring about a widespread and thorough knowledge of the principles which underlie the art of natation.

QUEMCUNQUE MISERUM VIDERIS HOMINEM SCIAS
Whomsoever you see in distress, recognise in him a fellow man

THE ROYAL LIFE SAVING SOCIETY

ITS AIMS AND TASK

The Task

The Royal Life Saving Society was formed in 1891 to reduce the annual toll of 2000 lives lost in drowning accidents in the United Kingdom by publicising the causes of these accidents, by encouraging everyone to learn to swim and by teaching competent swimmers individual methods of rescuing a drowning person. Despite a far greater use of water for recreation today, the number of deaths from drowning has been reduced to less than 1000 annually : but this is still too heavy a toll.

Aims and Scope

The work of the Society stems from the original aims, set out on the opposite page, and consists of three main parts : the teaching of water safety, the teaching of individual rescue methods and the provision of rescue teams (life guards). The preparation and training required provide excellent and purposeful physical recreation. Resuscitation forms an important part of life-saving instruction and is also taught as a separate subject. Volunteers carry on the work throughout the United Kingdom and in many Commonwealth countries for which the United Kingdom National Branch is responsible.

Proficiency Awards

An attempt at rescue by an untrained would-be rescuer, whose skill does not match his courage, may end in a double tragedy. *Proper teaching and testing are very important.* There are a series of graded tests to measure the standard achieved and to prepare for the advanced tests. Over 6,000,000 tests have been taken successfully since 1891 and the yearly total is increasing steadily. But this increase must continue until every competent swimmer is a trained life saver.

Individual Life Saving

The main work of the Society is the teaching of individual life saving methods. Seventy-five per cent of drowning accidents occur in places such as canals, rivers, gravel pits, etc. which can never be fully supervised or protected, and an individual acting on his own initiative and without aids may well be the only one capable of preventing a tragedy.

Water Safety

Putting over the need for water safety to the general public, and particularly the young, is an important task. Many are drowned before they have the chance of learning to swim and a special water safety proficiency test has been introduced to help with this problem and to show how even a non-swimmer can give some help in an emergency. The other two Safety Award tests measure individual swimming ability before participation in water sports and introduce the personal skills required for life saving.

Life Guard Corps

Qualified life savers can give a voluntary service to the community by joining the R.L.S.S. Life Guard Corps and carrying out patrols at weekends at popular coastal and inland bathing places. More information about the Life Guard Corps and its expanding service is given on page 126.

Mountbatten Medal

The recognition of bravery or efficiency in the saving of life is the prerogative of the Royal Humane Society, but the Royal Life Saving Society has the privilege of awarding the Mountbatten Medal annually to the holder of one of the Society's proficiency awards who performs the best rescue from drowning during the year.

Competitions

The Society recognises the value of competitions as a stimulus to interest and efficiency and enters teams for the International Life Saving Championships.

Membership and Aid

A strong membership and sound financial support are vital for expansion. The Society acknowledges the tremendous work done by its voluntary helpers, and the assistance and help given by the Department of Education and Science and the Local Authorities.

The Quarterly Journal keeps members in touch.

Co-operation
The Society believes that real co-operation between all the organisations working in the field of water safety is essential.

THE HANDBOOK

This latest edition of the Handbook has been thoroughly revised and brought up to date. It concentrates on realism and simplicity. It seeks to bridge the gap as much as possible between the teaching pool and its calm water conditions and open water where much more difficult conditions may be found. New methods such as the defensive skills are introduced, old and proved methods are kept but those which only duplicate have been discarded. Notes on teaching have been included for the first time.

With its improved layout and illustration the Handbook should serve as a useful basis for simplified and effective teaching and training. Use has been made of the other R.L.S.S. publications to avoid overloading the Handbook. For instance, notes on simple resuscitation only are included here: the more advanced resuscitation teaching is given in the R.L.S.S. Resuscitation Handbook. There is an Examiners Manual and a Life Guard Pamphlet. General administration is dealt with in a separate manual.

This Handbook shows:

the size of the drowning problem and the reason for the Society's existence;

an analysis of the cause of drowning accidents and the water safety rules which can prevent them;

the actions which can be taken when an accident happens and need for assessment as to the particular action required;

the swimming rescue skills required and how they should be taught;

the graduated tests which measure the degree of skill acquired;

matters of general interest about the Society.

After reading the water safety advice and learning the rescue methods and techniques, the Society hopes that the reader will be a safer swimmer and capable of helping others.

WATER SAFETY

CAUSES OF DROWNING ACCIDENTS

Nearly 1000 lives are lost annually in the United Kingdom, mainly from the following causes:

(1) Inadequate supervision, particularly of young children playing in or around water.

(2) Incorrect use of swimming supports in open water.

(3) Spirit of adventure, e.g. raft building, rock and cliff climbing, cave exploring, playing on ice.

(4) Unskilled or careless use of light water craft in deep water, tidal waters and currents.

(5) Bathing near rocks or in unfamiliar places where there are underwater dangers, such as a sudden change of depth.

(6) Swimming, boating, wading or fishing *alone*, often in remote places.

(7) Ignorance or disregard of strong currents, tides and undertows.

(8) "Showing off". Swimming out to off-shore boat or buoy, or across a river, or out to sea, for a "dare", when the return journey may be beyond the swimmer's capacity.

(9) Under-estimation of distance in open water and over-estimation of swimming skill.

(10) Multiple fatalities caused by persons, who are untrained or whose skill does not match their courage, going to the help of someone in distress.

The effect of cold and exposure may be an aggravating factor in any drowning accident.

An analysis of fatal drowning accidents which occurred in 1967 is given on page 136.

THE DANGERS OF OPEN WATER

Most swimming is done in swimming pools, where comparatively safe conditions exist.

But

by seaside, lake, river and other open water numerous dangers will be met:

tides, currents and ground swells;

sudden changes in water depth, unmarked and often unseen;

varying beds of sea, river and lake;

pits, pot-holes, stumps, rocks and mud to upset the balance;

cloudy water and weeds — particularly slippery seaweed;

winds, rough waves and surf;

cliffs, tide-bound coves and inlets;

often little or no supervision;

no life-guard patrols or few people about to raise the alarm and give assistance.

Main danger: ignorance, inexperience and over-confidence.

ENJOY YOUR LEISURE — RESPECT OPEN WATERS

PREVENTION OF ACCIDENTS

Advice for Those Looking After Young Children

TEACH THEM, WATCH OVER THEM AND TAKE COMMON SENSE PRECAUTIONS

The Problem

Children's natural curiosity and lack of fear.

Three or four inches of water is enough to drown a small child.

Hazards in and around The Home

Water butts should be covered; garden ponds and paddling pools should be securely fenced; sinks, baths, tubs and the like should be kept empty.

Always supervise children at play near water

Streams, Canals, Rivers, Gravel Pits near Home

Secure garden gates, fences and doors, and keep in good repair. Water is a great attraction **But** slippery and crumbling banks, weeds, loose or slippery stones can cause loss of balance. Ask the Local Authority or owners to fence dangerous waters.

Required — MAXIMUM SUPERVISION

House Boats and Yachts

To prevent falling overboard by slipping or climbing they should have:

    (a) secure guard rails, with netting for small children;

    (b) restricted window and door openings.

All children on deck must wear life jackets, and very young ones be attached to life lines.

TEACH THEM YOUNG

Very young children can be taught water confidence through supervised play. At the earliest opportunity they should be taught the rules of water safety and to swim. The Amateur Swimming Association and Swimming Teachers Association organise swimming instruction and can advise on the many good swimming manuals which are available.

Advice for Paddlers, Non-Swimmers and Weak Swimmers

(1)   Watch for pot-holes, quicksands and soft mud, especially around low tide.

(2)   In tidal waters do not paddle or wade to sandbanks or around rocky headlands, and do not explore coves and caves. Retreat can be quickly cut off by an incoming tide. If this happens, unless someone recognises the danger and calls out the rescue services, those cut off may drown.

(3)   Do ensure that air beds, rings and other types of floats are restricted by a line held by a responsible person or secured to some fixed point ashore. If not secured, currents, tides and winds can carry them into deep water. Do not take them beyond waist

depth, and then only in places where you can get a good foot-hold. Never over-load them.

(4) Do not venture into rivers, lakes, ponds, canals or gravel pits. Many have irregular, steep or slippery edges and varying depths near the sides. They are all potentially dangerous.

To Paddle or Bathe in Safety

Never bathe alone. Do not go into water deeper than waist level.
Never bathe just after a meal or when hungry. Do not skylark in or near water. Do not run on wet surrounds. Children should only enter the water with the permission of those in charge, and should stay within their sight.

> If in difficulty :
>
> keep calm ;
> call for help ;
> float on back ;
> wave **one** arm only to attract attention.

Advice for All Swimmers

On all occasions :

(1) Find out about bathing conditions and where and when it is safe to swim (reliable local sources include the Town Information Office, police and beach superintendents). Do not bathe when a **red flag** is flying.

(2) Bathe only in the centre area of a beach or in an area marked by red and yellow life-guard flags — **not** in secluded or remote coves or near rocks. Never swim near outfalls, sluices, bridges, wrecks or piers.

(3)   Do not stay too long in the water, especially if it is cold.

(4)   Do not wade out or swim above waist depth when a ground-swell or sea is running. The sudden surging mass of water sweeping to shore and returning seawards can unbalance both non-swimmers and swimmers and sweep them quickly out of depth, preventing their return. This is a major danger on surf coasts.

(5)   Do not run, jump or chase others on the side of a bath, lido or pool. A slip can injure the runner or anyone else with whom he collides.

(6)   Make certain that other swimmers are clear before jumping or diving into the water.

(7)   Do not duck others. It is easy to destroy the water confidence of a learner or nervous bather.

(8)   Do not skylark in deep water.

(9)   Take heed of warning notices. Do not hang clothes over, or otherwise obscure them.

(10)   Bathe with company — never alone.

(11)   When in open water swim parallel to and near the shore line. It is dangerous to swim straight out from shore or bank. Your safe return may be endangered by fatigue, cramp, ebb tide, currents or boats.

(12) When surf-riding or "shooting" waves take care to avoid collisions and bathers when there is no marked area for surfing.

(13) To avoid being submerged or knocked over by heavy surf or breakers learn to dive through the waves as they approach.

(14) Do not dive into water unless you know the depth and what lies below the surface.

(15) Do not chase a beach ball or other object being carried or blown out to sea. You may go too far for a safe return.

(16) Keep clear of the propellers of powered boats.

Advice for Water Craft Users

General Rules

(1) Get to know local conditions — rise and fall of tides, currents, shoals, indication of sudden weather changes, etc. (local boatmen, fishermen, coastguards, police, harbour-masters, beach-masters or life guards will help).

(2) Do not go boating if you cannot swim at least 50 yards in the clothing usually worn for the activity.

(3) For small boat activities wear a life-jacket or buoyancy aid which conforms to the standards of the Board of Trade, British Standards Institute or the Ship and Boat Builders National Federation.

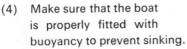

(4) Make sure that the boat is properly fitted with buoyancy to prevent sinking.

(5) Never wear wellingtons (gum-boots) afloat. In the water these are difficult to get off, fill with water and drag you down.

(6) Never overload a boat. Never fool about in one.

(7) If boating alone, leave word ashore where you are going; take extra care.

(8) Early and late in the year the water is cold and rescuers are few. In very cold water consciousness can be lost quickly.

(9) In the event of a capsize **stay with the boat**, secure yourself to it if you can and keep your clothes on. A boat can be seen more easily than a swimmer.

(10) Practise capsize drill when the weather is fine.

(11) If bad weather threatens, make at once for shelter. Warning signs are:

    (i) rising wind;

    (ii) waves increase in size and "white horses" appear;

    (iii) sky becomes overcast (leaden) to windward.

(12) Read *Water Wisdom,* published by "B.P" for the Royal Yachting Association, and learn the "rules of the road".

Small Sailing Boats and Canoes

In addition to the above:

(1) Get proper training from the Royal Yachting Association or British Canoe Union.

(2) Keep clear of other craft.

(3) Keep away from weirs, tide rips and rocks.

(4) Do not attempt to change places in a canoe or dinghy.

(5) Do not go on fast rivers without proper training.

(6) Do not attempt to right a capsized canoe. The air trapped inside helps to keep it afloat.

(7) Stow all gear correctly, so that it will not impede the canoeist.

Powered Boats

Take great care when swimmers are about. Keep clear of propellers. Think carefully before climbing aboard from the water; outboard motors sometimes prevent entry over the stern, usually the most suitable place, and small speedboats are very unstable when stationary.

Rubber Dinghies

If using single-handed, fix a trailing life line. Wind can blow them away much faster than a man can swim.

Rafts

Do not make rafts for use in deep water except under expert supervision.

Unless the raft is quite stable do not attempt to climb on to it from the water.

Advice for Fishermen, Especially Children

(1)   Avoid fishing alone.

(2)   Choose your fishing site with care to avoid :

    (a)   steep, weak or crumbling banks ;

    (b)   being cut off by the tide or knocked over and swept away by a sudden wave, which, even in calm conditions, may appear without warning.

(3)   Good balance and secure foothold are vital. Sloping and slippery rocks are perilous, especially with unsuitable footwear.

Do not overload the boat!

(4)   When fishing from a boat :

    (a)   follow the general rules given on page 18 ;

    (b)   do not stand in a small boat to play or land a fish ;

    (c)   do not crowd to one side to watch.

(5) Underwater fishing is highly specialised and requires proper training by the British Sub Aqua Club or local underwater swimming club. Use properly tested and approved equipment: other equipment is often dangerous.

USEFUL KNOWLEDGE

Study the Behaviour of Water

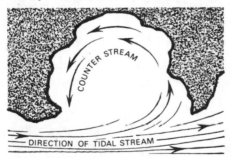

COUNTER STREAM

DIRECTION OF TIDAL STREAM

Tides rise vertically, and the tidal stream flows along the shore. In Britain the rising (flood) tide moves towards the English Channel. The falling (ebb) tide moves away from the English Channel. Waves caused by winds seldom bring water straight on to the beach although they appear to do so.

In an enclosed bay a current may circulate in the opposite direction to the main flood stream.

In a tidal river, estuary or inlet the incoming water, pushing against gravity, takes the longest route uphill so that the current is at strongest and the water

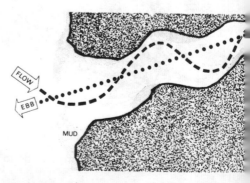

FLOW

EBB

MUD

deepest at the outside of the bends. There will be slack, shallower water or eddies on the inside bends.

The outgoing water takes the shortest route downhill close to the inside bends. Slack water will be found on the outside bends.

Fresh water meeting salt water drops as mud any soil it is carrying. Mud caused by the incoming tide is thickest on the inside bends. Fresh water flowing out on the ebb meets salt water off-shore and makes a mud bar there.

Fast-flowing fresh water causes turbulence at the point where it meets the tide commencing to rise.

Water flowing into a cove or bay is squeezed by the land and flows fastest at the sides and corners, both coming in and going out.

How to Tell the Direction of Tidal Stream or Current

Look for ripples, streaming away from fixed objects, buoys tilted over by water, moored boats lying to the current. But do not rely solely on boats because if they have shallow keels and the wind is strong, they will tend to lie partly to the wind rather than to the current.

Moored or Fixed Obstructions in a Stream

In deep water where a tidal stream or current is flowing, water has to flow past obstructions. In so doing it increases speed. This often creates a powerful suction or pressure at the upstream end, which can pin a swimmer or drag him under.

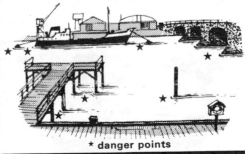

★ danger points

Barges sometimes have chains slung below them, and moored vessels have anchor or mooring chains against which swimmers can be trapped.

Keep well clear of the upstream end of any moored boat or obstruction. This advice also applies to users of small boats and canoes.

Sea Cliffs

Most sea cliffs are largely loose rock and soil. Do not climb them unless you are part of an experienced team with proper equipment.

A climber starting from the foot of the cliff at low tide may be cut off as the tide rises. Climbing down from the top is difficult. If a climber falls into deep water, he may be unable to land and may be thrown against the rocks.

ACTION IN DANGEROUS SITUATIONS

You have been warned to avoid dangerous situations, but the following notes will help to prepare you for the unexpected accident.

When Thrown Suddenly into Deep Water

In an accident to a pleasure boat, for instance, you may be thrown suddenly into deep water fully clothed.

Get hold of a support if possible (lifebelt, wreckage, etc.).
Remove wellingtons, waders, boots or shoes.
Take off heavy clothing — overcoats, jackets, etc.
Keep on other clothing to help you keep warm and afloat.
Do not panic.
Call for help.
Try to attract attention by waving clothing or one arm only. (In a patrolled area the signal for help is one arm held straight up.)

Far from shore

Conserve energy and body heat by minimum movement.

Use any available support. With no support, float on back.

Clothing can be used to trap air and support a person in the water. It can be blown up to make floats. This needs swimming ability and practice.

Knot clothes so that there is only one air opening, for example tie knots in the bottom of trouser legs. Inflate by waving quickly through the air or by scooping air and water by hand into the opening from the surface. The water will leak away and the air be trapped. The air will leak slowly from the clothing, so that it has to be topped up by repeating the operation or by blowing air through the material. Do not lean too heavily on inflated clothes as they will leak more quickly if pushed below the surface.

Many methods are possible; experiment with different garments.

Near Shore

If you have a support it may be wise to await rescue. If not, it may be necessary to swim for shore. For longer distances:

Undress.

Gauge the current and swim with or diagonally across it.

Use breast, back or side stroke to conserve energy.

Try occasional feet first dives to test depth.

In a River

Assess the best place to make landfall considering state of bank, bends, etc. Swim diagonally across the current.

Quicksand or Deep Mud

Do not try to stand up and walk. Lie flat on the surface and move by a slow breast stroke action.

Underwater Weeds

Swim very gently with a long, slow breast or side stroke with minimum leg movement. Weeds will float apart: never fight them.

Weirs

AVOID WEIRS. If drawn over one, swim hard to reach the bottom. Tuck your body into a ball and hold your breath until thrown to the surface well down stream. Do not try to reach the surface quickly or you will be caught in the standing wave or "stopper" below the weir.

Fast and Rocky Rivers

It is dangerous to ford a river when it is in flood or in mountainous country. If it is absolutely *necessary* to cross, **find a bridge** if possible. If you must enter the water, avoid the narrowest point. Look for a wide part where the water will usually be shallowest. Avoid a stretch above a waterfall or rocks. Make sure before starting that there is a good landfall. Use a pole or staff to feel  your way. Plant it ahead before taking a step and lean against the current.

Motor Cars falling into Water

To avoid this, park *parallel* to the water's edge on jetties, docks and piers, etc.

If you are in a sinking vehicle — **keep calm.**

(1) Wind up all windows.

(2) Switch on lights to guide rescuers.

(3) Do **not** try to open doors.

(4) Lift up children into the air pocket.

(5) When the water reaches the chin, the pressure inside and out will be equalised. Take a deep breath and try to force the door open. If this fails, try to kick out the windscreen.

(6) If there are more than one in the car, link hands and go out in a human chain to make sure no one is left behind.

Surf

If carried away and there are no patrols to help, swim towards the shore in troughs of large waves until they begin to break. Then try to surf in on top of a wave. When you touch the sand, dig your hands into it to anchor yourself against the undertow; then go forward with the next wave. Scramble above high-water mark.

Ice

Young children should be kept off ice-covered ponds, canals, gravel pits etc., unless parents or responsible adults are there to see that they are safe. Even if the ice appears to be safe, there is always danger unless the depth of water beneath is less than the waist height of the smallest child present. If anyone falls through and the stream carries him under the ice, he may be beyond help unless he can break through. Ice is seldom the same thickness over any area. It is normally thickest and strongest close to the shore. Remember that new ice melts quickly.

If you have fallen through, call for help. Move towards safety with arms spread across the surface of the ice, breaking it as you go. If it proves strong enough to support you, kick to a swimming position and slide forward on to the ice. Remain lying on the ice and work your way to safety.

How to Help

A rescuer should avoid going onto weakened ice. Try to reach the victim with a pole or rope and pull him to safety.

If you have to go across the ice to help him, use a ladder, plank, human chain lying down or other methods of spreading the rescuer's weight over the surface of the ice. Move with caution.

First-aid measures are urgent. Resuscitation and Aftercare are covered in Sections IV and V respectively.

PREVENTION IS BETTER THAN CURE

Non-Swimmers

Learn the water safety rules. Learn how to help others.
Learn simple resuscitation.

QUALIFY FOR THE WATER SAFETY AWARD

This proficiency award has been introduced specially for inexperienced and non-swimmers, particularly the young. The conditions and the appropriate water safety rules are set out on page 89. Practise can take place in any large hall or playground. All children who are not proficient swimmers should qualify for this test.

Everyone should learn simple resuscitation as described in Section IV. Hundreds of lives are saved each year by this means.

LEARN TO SWIM

A few yards can be the difference between life and death.

Inexperienced Swimmers

Swim regularly. Learn various strokes.
Strengthen your swimming by increasing the distances.
Practise water skills and resuscitation.

QUALIFY FOR THE WATER SAFETY AWARD AND
THE SAFETY AWARDS

The R.L.S.S. Preliminary and Advanced Safety Awards were introduced in 1963 to provide a test by which people of all ages can prove their ability to look after themselves in an accident in or on water and so avoid being a liability to others. The Society had particularly in mind the need to provide a standard for use by sailing clubs, canoe clubs and similar organisations to prove a member's competence in this respect before taking part in club activities. The personal skills required are an introduction to life saving. Details of these personal skills are given on page 42, and the conditions of the awards on page 92.

Average Swimmers

Practise regularly and so make yourself a better swimmer.
Learn three or four strokes well. Swim longer distances.
Become "at home" in the water. Observe the water safety rules.

QUALIFY FOR THE SAFETY AWARDS

Strong Swimmers

Swim regularly.
Learn and practise water skills and life saving skills.
Join a life-saving class or a life-guard club.

QUALIFY FOR THE LIFE-SAVING AWARDS

Water skills and life-saving skills (rescue and resuscitation), are dealt
with in later sections.

PRINCIPLES AND METHODS OF RESCUE

PRINCIPLES

WATCHFULNESS   ASSESSMENT   ACTION

Watchfulness

Drowning accidents happen suddenly. They are not expected. A trained rescuer, because he is alert, recognises someone in distress. He may see :

a swimmer, in spite of great effort, making little or no headway in trying to return to land ;

someone disappearing and reappearing ;

a child or an apparent non-swimmer on an airbed drifting seawards, or downstream, out of control ;

an indifferent swimmer chasing a float or ball out to sea and swimming into danger.

Assessment

THINK BEFORE YOU ACT

Whatever the degree of skill of the person who recognises a dangerous situation, a swift assessment of the situation is vital ; otherwise the wrong action may be taken with possibly fatal results. (e.g., starting to swim a long distance, when a boat is available).

These are some of the factors which affect the plan of action :

degree of urgency ;

numbers in danger ;

your own skill and experience ;

help available — people (degree of competence) — boats — rescue aids ;

distance from bank or shore ;

strength and direction of current ;

strength of wind and waves ;

hazards in or under the water ;

depth of the water ;

entry and landing places.

Time spent on assessment may vary from almost instant assessment (reaching out to grasp someone) to the making of a deliberate plan (people cut off by the tide but not yet in immediate danger). All that may be necessary is to inform a life guard. All that may be possible is to shout or run for help (when you realise that a personal rescue is beyond your own capabilities — do not make it a double tragedy).

Assessment of a situation is very important and is included in the life saving examinations. No two situations are exactly alike and therefore the action required will differ. After reading this section pose to yourself different situations and consider the best action for each.

Action

Once the plan is made, action must be decisive and speedy. Reassessment during action will be necessary so that adjustments can be made (the unexpected approach of a rescue boat may enable a rescuer of limited ability to apply resuscitation at once; or the strength of the current may compel him to abandon the attempt).

Action should be simultaneous when there are helpers — while one person attempts the rescue, another can alert Beach Rescue Headquarters (if there is one) or the lifeguard or the police or ambulance, according to circumstances.

METHODS

The following methods of individual rescue action should be considered in this order: REACH — THROW — WADE — ROW — SWIM taking a support — SWIM and TOW.

Everyone can give help in some way. A weak or non-swimmer can REACH, THROW or WADE. He can go for help. He can assist in resuscitation and after-care.

Assessment   ## Action

When the victim is near the bank, etc.

Try to REACH him

When farther out

THROW a rope or support

When some way out in shallow water

WADE to reach or throw

When a long way out

ROW if possible (or use a powered boat)

Otherwise, provided you can swim well

SWIM taking a support

(if you can't

fetch help)

Or if a trained life saver, as a last resort

SWIM and TOW

WARNING

The approach to a victim must be made with great caution to avoid his clutch, which can be vice-like through fear.

1. Reach

Anchorage

Lie flat on the bank. Grasp the victim with one hand: hold on to something secure with the other, if possible.

Extended Reach

Extend your natural reach by using a branch, pole, oar or clothing.

Human Chain

Rescuers face alternately in opposite directions and grasp the inside of each other's wrists securely. Extend the chain by adding links at the *shore* end.

The anchor man should be secured throughout. This method applies especially to shallow beaches and rivers.

2. Throw

Supports (Buoyant Aids)

A swimming ring, life belt, surf board, plank, beach ball or other buoyant object can be thrown to, or slid along the surface of the water to, the victim. Launch flat objects with the leading edge higher than the trailing edge to skim the surface.

Air beds should only be used when there is no wind or nothing else available.

A line attachment is an advantage.

AIM TO ONE SIDE of the victim to avoid injury and up current if in moving water. Allow for wind.

Rope

When using a hand line divide the coils between both hands, with most coils in the throwing hand. Quickly anchor the end if possible or hold it securely in the other hand: hold the coils in this hand loosely to let the rope pay out.

Aim beyond and a little to the side of the victim but within his reach and up current if in moving water. Allow for wind.

In recovery keep the end of the rope high to give lift to the victim. Haul steadily, but not fast enough to submerge the victim or pull the rope out of his hands.

Practise all these skills, in particular:

(a) throwing a line in any open space aiming at a definite point some 20 yards away;

(b) gliding a plank of wood into the water from a height of 3 to 6 feet to obtain correct angle of impact.

3. Wade

This lengthens "reach" or "throw" as it brings the rescuer nearer the victim. Wade up to thigh depth watching for underwater obstructions. Grasp the victim rather than allow him to grasp you. Keep a firm foot-hold and lean backwards.

4. Row

If a boat is available, provided it is seaworthy and the rescuer able to handle it, this may prove the quickest and safest method for longer rescues. Boats left on shore are often chained up and without oars : so do not count on being able to use them.

If a helper is available a team of two will be much more effective.

Approach

Take care in approaching, particularly if the boat is small enough for the victim to capsize it. Drift the stern down to the victim and instruct him to hold on. Do not rush to get him aboard if he is conscious but if there is a rope on board use it to secure him under the armpits.

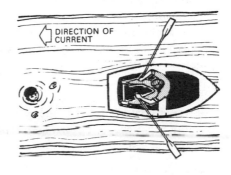

If the victim is unconscious and floating, again secure him if possible. Give resuscitation before attempting to lift him aboard.

If the victim has sunk, do not dive from the boat as this will push it away. Lower yourself into the water over the stern. When you have recovered the victim, use the boat as a support to give resuscitation before trying to board.

Getting Aboard

In general people are brought aboard at any place where the boat is stable. In a small dinghy this will usually be over the stern. Pull up the victim far enough to get his trunk into the boat, push head and shoulders down as low as possible then get the lower body and legs aboard.

Getting the victim from the water or re-entering the boat with him may prove impossible if the boat is small, unstable or the victim fully clothed. In this case hold on until help comes.

35

With a team of two time can be saved if one rescuer remains in the water holding on to boat and victim, while the other rows.

General

Boat rescues are complicated by wind, waves, tides and currents. The rescuer must constantly assess how, or even whether, he can cope with the prevailing conditions.

In most conditions a boat can be propelled faster than any rescuer could swim and will provide a better chance of an effective rescue.

If the boat is capsized during a rescue bring the victim to it and use it as a support. Learn the skills of boat handling and practise rescues from boats.

Powered Boats

A powered boat in skilled hands will be more effective than a rowing boat in a long rescue, but the stern approach can only be done with the propeller still.

5. Swim Taking a Support

It may be sufficient to swim out with a support (lifebelt etc). if one is to hand and when boat or other assistance is likely to become available. **Physical contact must be avoided** when the support is offered to the victim. With a conscious victim the rescuer will stand by until help comes, giving encouragement. If unconscious, a support such as the torpedo buoy can be secured to the victim or used to support both.

If anything goes wrong, this method then merges with the next, Swim and Tow, provided the rescuer is fully qualified : if not qualified, it may be wiser for him to return alone to seek help.

6. Swim and Tow

Having decided that a swim and tow rescue is necessary, the rescuer has two main courses open to him, dependent on the distance from shore or bank:

Up to 20 yards: a quick dash, removing heavy top clothing and footwear only.

Beyond 20 yards: a swim without clothes, for which the delay in undressing is justified and necessary. If available and suitable for the particular circumstances a towing aid can be taken out.

SEQUENCE OF A SWIMMING RESCUE

PRE-ENTRY — ENTRY — SWIM OUT — APPROACH — CONTACT — TOW — LANDING   with repeated reassessment

Pre-Entry — Sighting and Cross Bearings

After making his plan in the case of a long swim the rescuer should remember the need to keep direction, for it may be difficult to keep the victim in sight all the time, particularly in rough water. Take a sighter, if possible, on a point beyond the victim. If there are others present, cross

bearings can be achieved by two or more persons spaced along the shore pointing continuously at the victim.

Entry

The rescuer's point of entry will affect safety, progress and speed. It may well be quicker to run a distance to a point nearest the victim or ahead of him from which you can cut him off, than to attempt a direct swim. Therefore the rescuer must assess the best point of entry.

POINT OF ENTRY

37

If the water conditions are unknown a cautious feet first entry is safest. If entry from a height is unavoidable, it should be feet first and as shallow as possible.

Wade, if possible, before starting to swim.

Swim Out

Try to keep the victim in sight. Good judgement is needed to balance the need for speed in the swim out and the need to conserve strength for the difficult tow back. Use your best stroke to achieve this. Back stroke should not be used — unless you do not have another strong stroke — as it is difficult to keep the victim in sight.

If at hand, swimming fins can be of great assistance to a rescuer who is used to them. Take care not to swim out farther than you can return, should the fins be lost.

Approach

Final approach to the victim should always be carried out with head up and great caution. Breast stroke is best at this stage. Towing aids

should be used to prevent contact. With no aid, defensive action should be used to avoid the victim's clutch. Throughout the approach the rescuer should calm and encourage a conscious victim to co-operate. If the victim is panic stricken the rescuer should keep away at a safe distance until his struggles lessen and it is safe to make contact *from behind*. Underwater search and recovery may be necessary.

If a towing aid has been taken, the victim will be offered one end. Contact between the rescuer and the victim is thus eliminated until a position of safety is reached. The towing aid can be quickly released if the victim "climbs" along it towards the rescuer.

38

Defence

If a clutch is attempted the rescuer must back away or parry, and keep off until it is safe to contact the victim from behind.

Contact

The moment of contact between the rescuer and the victim is the most dangerous point of any rescue. The rescuer must immediately seize the initiative in gaining control of the victim.

Should the victim obtain a clutch the rescuer must at all costs release himself by the method that will free him to survive and save the victim. This could mean delivering a blow or kick as a last resort. Releases are described on page 50.

Exhausted Swimmer

In the case of an exhausted swimmer who is likely to sink the rescuer should make contact at once — even at the risk of a clutch.

Submerged Victim

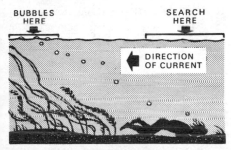

BUBBLES HERE

SEARCH HERE

DIRECTION OF CURRENT

If the victim disappears under water the rescuer must try to locate and retrieve him by a head- or feet-first surface dive and, if necessary, systematic search.

Bubbles may rise to the surface, indicating the victim's position. In still water

they rise vertically but in running water they are carried downstream, in which case the search should be carried out upstream of the point at which they appear.

Should the victim be lying on a hard bottom the rescuer should seize him under the armpits and push off vigorously from the bottom. If the bottom is muddy or otherwise dangerous, the rescuer should swim upwards, taking care not to touch the bottom.

39

The eyes must be kept open to assist the search and note dangers. A succession of short quick dives is better than a prolonged underwater swim, when there is a risk that the rescuer himself may lose consciousness.

Tow

This must give firm support to the victim and complete control to the rescuer.

The tow should be as direct as possible to the point of safety (not necessarily the closest landfall) and should keep the victim's face clear of the water at all times. Tows are described on page 53.

The victim should be towed to safety at best speed, i.e., the rescuer must balance the need for speed in the case of an unconscious victim with the distance and difficulty of the swim and of his own strength and skill.

Reel and Line

On some unmanned beaches reel and line (Hicks Box equipment) is provided. A team of two or more is necessary. There are simple instructions on the lid. The better swimmer puts on the belt and swims to the victim. The other man pays out the line.

When ready to be hauled in the rescuer signals with one arm raised vertically. The reel man then hauls in STEADILY. *There is danger in hauling too quickly* that rescuer and victim may be submerged. If this happens the rescuer should give the "stop hauling" signal (wave one arm from side to side).

The belt is provided with a quick release, should this be needed.

Landing

With an unconscious victim who is not breathing resuscitation should be given as soon as the rescuer has reached a secure position. This may be in shallow water or holding the side of a boat. Once landed the victim should receive continued resuscitation and aftercare as necessary.

Note: Resuscitation should be given to an unconscious victim who is not breathing at the earliest opportunity after contact — non-swimmers can be useful at this stage. Only a strong, experienced life saver should attempt it in deep water without support. For this reason the deep water technique is not introduced until the Award of Merit stage.

Re-assessment

The rescuer must re-assess the situation from time to time to determine if a change of plan is necessary.

Preparedness and Training

To be ready for a swimming rescue a rescuer must be properly trained and in practise. The best way of becoming proficient is to join a life-saving club or class and receive proper instruction before taking a proficiency test.

Training should be approached not only with the idea of passing a set examination but also with a view to becoming master of differing situations which might occur.

Once qualified the trained life saver should keep in practise by regularly taking a repeat test (bar) or by training for a higher test.

Training with others in staged incidents is invaluable.

It is wise to practise contact skills in the presence of a qualified life saver in case of accident.

PERSONAL SKILLS

The competent swimmer will need to learn these personal skills before learning the rescue skills set out at the end of this section. The Safety Awards are designed to test these personal skills.

Life Saving Back Stroke (Without Use of Arms)

Keep the upper part of the legs in line with the body. As the knees open sideways, lower the feet till they are below the former position of the knees. The movement is a short continuous circular action from the knees. The insteps and shins press against the resistance of the water. The continuous movement produces steady progress without jerking.

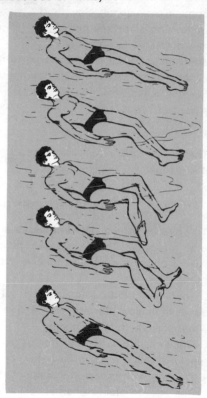

Side Stroke

The side stroke is less strenuous than most other strokes; so it can be kept up for longer distances, particularly when towing. The position of the rescuer's face allows regular breathing even in choppy water and allows him also to look ahead.

The Gliding Position:

The body is straight, lying on the side, with face resting in the water. The lower arm is fully extended beyond the head, palm of the hand downward. The upper arm is along the side of the body.

Arm Action:

From the glide position make the stroke with the lower arm by pulling

through the water with a shallow circular sweep beneath and back to the shoulder. At the same time move the upper arm to the forward position.

Glide the lower arm fully forward and at the same time, except when towing, make a backward pull with the upper arm just below the surface, finishing alongside the thigh.

Leg Action:

As the lower arm glides forward make a scissor kick parallel to the surface of the water.

Sculling

Lie on the back in the water. Keep the body horizontal but relaxed, hips up, legs together and toes pointed. Look towards the toes without raising the head.

For head-first sculling, keep the arms straight, close to and slightly below the sides of the body. Cup hands and push the water towards the feet with a continuous circular movement.

For feet-first sculling reverse the movement and push the water towards the head.

Treading Water

With body upright, keep nose and mouth above the water by normal leg movements.

In addition press down with palms against the water, with wrists turned outwards, using a sculling action. Keep the head tilted back in a comfortable position to keep nose and mouth clear of the water.

If the arms are raised from the water, you will sink.

Undressing in the Water

Generally speaking, clothes can be taken off in one of three ways:

(a) Jacket Fashion

Articles which unbutton fully down the front present little difficulty; take them off, while treading water, much as if on dry land.

(b) Over the Head

For those which come over the head, roll up closely under the armpits, then with one quick lift get the roll over the head.

Alternatively, remove one arm and roll up that side before lifting over the head.

Take special care when removing overhead clothing made of nylon type material to avoid covering the face. See the warning on page 85.

(c) Lowered from the Legs

For trousers, skirts, etc. which have to fall from the legs, undo the belt or other support and kick them off, while taking off upper garments; then help with the hands.

Surface Dives

(a) Head First

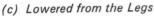

Swim to a position which is 6 feet short of the point immediately above the object to be recovered. Thrust arms vertically downwards and use

45

a breast stroke action to pull the body down. At the same time turn the head and shoulders sharply down into the water, bend quickly at the hips and lift straight legs clear of the water. This will bring the body into line and the weight of the legs above the water will help to take you down. Gain added depth by swimming.

(b) Feet First

Make this dive immediately over the object to be recovered. With body upright as low as possible in the water, give a strong breast stroke kick and press down with the hands to raise body high out of the water. Take a deep breath and as you descend sweep the arms sideways and upwards above the head. Point the toes and keep the legs together.

Jump Entries

(a) Straddle Jump—for Shallow Entry

Spring forward into the water with legs spread wide apart to the front and back. Flex the knees slightly and lean the trunk forward to an angle of about 40 degrees. Extend the arms sideways and slightly forward, elbows bent a little. Keep the head in line with the body.

DO NOT USE THIS ENTRY FROM HEIGHTS OVER ONE METRE

Compact Jump — For Entry from Height

Step forward and hold the legs together in line with the trunk. Flex the knees and ankles slightly. Hold the arms tightly to the side or cross them over the chest. As you hit the surface breathe out strongly through the nose. Slow the descent in the water by spreading the arms and kicking.

Leaving Deep Water Without Assistance

Use the lifting power of the water.
Place the hands on the edge and duck down. Make a breast stroke kick and pull up until the body is over the hands with arms straight. Lean forward. Get one leg sideways on the top and climb out.

47

RESCUE SKILLS

The skills included in this section will form the basis for ready action by the trained life saver, with variations according to the circumstances. The actions must be performed in a vigorous manner.

Defensive Methods

These skills are designed to allow the rescuer to "stand off" a dangerous subject or avoid a sudden clutch.

Reverse

The basic defensive technique to reverse the position of the body with rapidity and ease.

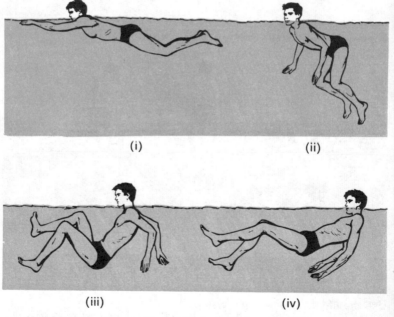

(i) (ii)

(iii) (iv)

From the prone swimming position, fling your head and shoulders back, tuck your knees towards your chest and scull backwards with arms and hands. Kick vigorously to move away from the subject.

Single Leg Block

If the subject is close enough to attempt a clutch, as you "reverse" block his attempt by thrusting against his chest or shoulder with one leg.

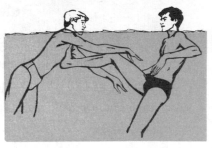

Counter

If your leg is grasped, tread the subject under water until he is below you. When his head is level with your waist, take him by the chin and turn him into a towing position.

Duck Away

To avoid a sudden clutch at close quarters immediately lower your head and push upwards with your hands against his hips, waist, chest or arms, forcing him away. Speed and aggression are essential.

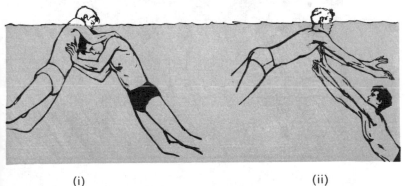

(i)   (ii)

Releases

Should the rescuer fail to avoid a clutch an immediate vigorous release is vital. In all cases care should be taken to maintain control of and contact with the subject immediately after the release has been made.

Front Clutch Round Neck or Body

Used when the rescuer is seized from the front in any position.

Push Away Break

(a) If the head and neck are clutched, drop the chin and exert leverage on the subject's elbows or upper arms or under his arm pits.

(b) If a pinion clutch, force your elbows outwards and upwards and grasp the subject under the armpits or on his trunk. Take a

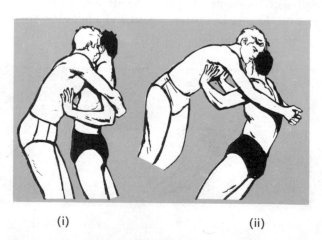

(i)   (ii)

deep breath and slip out of his clutch by submerging with your chin tucked well into your shoulder. While submerged turn the subject to a towing position.

Wrist Grip

Used when the rescuer's wrist or arm is clutched by both hands of the subject.

(a) Pull Control

Pull the subject towards you with the gripped arm; swing your free arm round the back of the subject's neck, taking a firm grip on his chin. At the same time give a powerful leg kick raising yourself above and behind him. In this position you may be able to pull your arm free; if not the subject can still be towed easily by the chin.

(b) Arm Pull

Used if "pull control" cannot be effected.

Clench the fist of the gripped arm. With your free arm reach over or under, according to the grip, between the subject's arms. Take hold

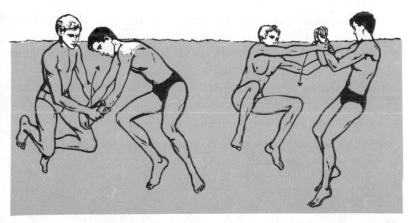

of the clenched fist and pull up or down, applying pressure against his thumb joints. There is a momentary loss of contact, so re-establish control immediately by grasping and turning him into a towing position.

Back Clutch Round Neck or Body

When the rescuer is seized from behind in any position he must immediately protect his throat by forcing his chin down.

(a) Elbow Break

Used against clutches above the rescuer's elbows.

Drop the chin. Grasp one of his wrists with your opposite hand and his elbow with your other hand. Then force the elbow up and pull

downwards and inwards on his wrist. Turn your head away from the elbow you are forcing up and duck underneath his arm, holding on to his wrist until you have turned it behind his back. Keep it there until you have him in a towing position.

(b) Joint Pressure Break

Used against clutches pinning the rescuer's elbows.

Grip the subject's thumbs or fingers and force his hands apart by pressure against the joints.

Separation of Two Swimmers Locked Together

Approach the weaker swimmer, if known, from behind. Grip his chin with both hands and bear down on him with your forearms, submerging both subjects. Bring one foot over the subject's locked arms, place it on the chest of the subject you are not holding and thrust them apart. At the same time pull the subject you are holding up and back.

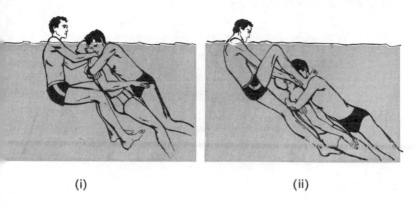

(i)   (ii)

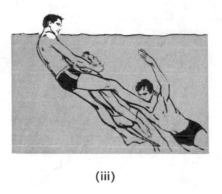

(iii)

Tows

The rescuer should use in each case the method best suited to himself and to the conditions. In all tows remember to keep the subject's face clear of the water.

Extended Tow

Used with a passive or co-operative subject.

Cup the subject's chin or grip his hair or loose clothing behind his neck, and tow him with your arm extended. Use side stroke or life saving back stroke.

Chin Tow

Used with a subject needing firm control.

From behind pass your arm over the subject's shoulder. Cup his chin in your hand with his head turned into your shoulder. Secure a firm grip by pressing your arm into his shoulder. Use your free arm to help you swim.

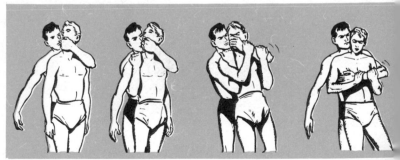

Shoulder Restraint
If the subject struggles, pass your free arm under his armpit and take a firm grip on his shoulder from the front.

54

Breathing Restraint

If the shoulder restraint does not control the subject, grip his nose and cover his mouth with the hand cupping his chin, to stop him breathing. He will then instinctively pull your arm down onto his chest and hold it there; try to grip him under the armpit to secure your hold. The tow can continue in this position, and you may be able to resume swimming with the arm which has been applying the shoulder restraint.

Cross Chest Tow

Used in rough or difficult conditions with the side stroke.

Place one arm over the subject's shoulder across his chest, clamping your elbow firmly down, and grasp him under the opposite armpit. While swimming keep your upper hip close to the small of his back.

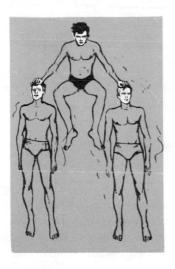

If the subject struggles, place your free hand under his armpit and pull his shoulder firmly against your chest.

Double Rescue Tow

In favourable conditions it is possible for an expert life saver to tow two subjects at once, by the hair, clothes or chin provided they are co-operative or passive. The rescuer grasps one subject with each hand and swims on his back.

Landing and Carrying a Rescued Person

The "Support" Position
Used to secure the subject in a position of safety against a firm support with his face out of the water.

From behind, pass your arms under the subject's armpits and secure him with a firm grip on bar, side or other support such as boat, steep bank, landing stage.

Walk Out
As soon as you can stand, hold the subject under the armpits and walk backwards, floating him.

Landing — Subject First

The Stirrup Method
Used when the subject is able to help and can be assisted out first.

Support him against the side. Reach down, cupping your free hand for his foot or bent lower leg. Lift him on to the top. When in shallow water, if he does not need to be supported, use both hands to make the stirrup.

Landing — Rescuer First

When the subject is unable to help, the rescuer places the subject's hands on the top one above the other, holding him there with his face above the water while climbing out.

There are two methods of getting the subject out unaided.

(a) The Crossed Arm Method
When you are out of the

water, cross your arms and hold the subject's wrists. Lift him up and down two or three times, bending and straightening your knees. Take care to keep his face above the water. Then lift him from the water uncrossing your arms as you do so. This will bring him into a sitting position facing the water. Take great care to avoid injuring the subject against the side as you lift. Protect his head if you lie him down.

(b) The Straight Arm Method

In *deep water* the preparatory movements are the same as above. Without crossing your arms grip the subject's wrists and lift him up and over the edge so that he rests on his chest. With one hand firmly on his back to secure him, use your other hand to lift his legs on to the side.

In *shallow water* this method can be used without the preparatory movements. *With caution*, lift the subject up and fold him gently over the edge. Avoid bumping his head as you lower him.

If you are not able to lift his legs on to the side from this position, get back into the water to do so.

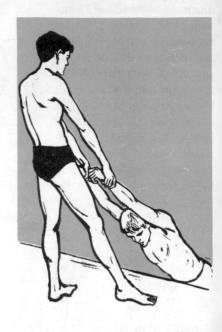

Carry

If it is necessary to carry the subject ashore unaided, the Fireman's Lift is one method which can be used. However, much will depend on how tired the rescuer is and the weight of the subject. There is risk of injury to both if he fails in the lift.

The Fireman's Lift

When the water is level with your hips, float the subject, face upwards between yourself and the land. Grasp the subject's nearest wrist with one hand and pass your other hand over and under his near thigh. Duck your head under his waist and roll him across your shoulders: then stand up lifting him clear of the water. Make this whole movement quickly, as the subject's face may be momentarily under water. Transfer the subject's wrist to the hand which you have passed round his thigh, leaving one arm free.

To lower the subject bend at the knees and hips to allow his feet to rest on the ground. Support the subject's weight, slip your head from under his arm and grasp him around his sides and back. Step backwards lowering him onto his knees. Move your hands up under his armpits and moving backwards lower him carefully to the ground.

RESUSCITATION

Resuscitation is the essential first-aid treatment required by the victim of any accident which restricts the intake of oxygen. It must be applied without any delay if it is to be successful.

Golden Rules:

(1) Keep calm.
(2) Get air into the lungs by starting resuscitation immediately.
(3) Send for help.

RESPIRATION AND THE CIRCULATION OF BLOOD

Elementary knowledge of the working of those parts of the body concerned with respiration and the circulation of blood will help the trained life saver to understand more fully how and why methods of resuscitation will be effective.

Every cell of the body needs oxygen for survival and will be damaged and eventually die without it. The cells of the brain are damaged especially quickly by a shortage of oxygen. This is why it is so important to start resuscitation as soon as possible after normal respiration has stopped, whatever the cause.

Air, which is composed of one-fifth oxygen, enters the body through the mouth and nose and passes through the throat into the windpipe. The upper part of the windpipe is protected by a special flap, which allows the entry of air but prevents the entry of other materials, such as food or water, etc.

Passing down the windpipe, air enters the lungs which, with the heart and largest blood vessels (arteries and veins), are protected by the ribs, which form the strong cage of the chest. In the lungs oxygen passes from the air into the blood and carbon dioxide from the blood into the air in the lungs, to be breathed out.

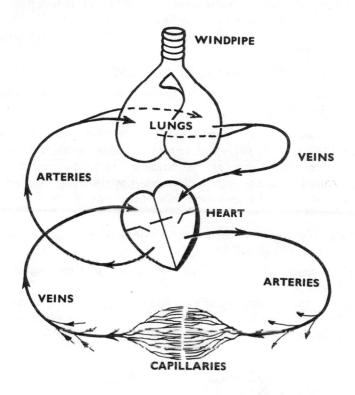

WINDPIPE

LUNGS

VEINS

ARTERIES

HEART

ARTERIES

VEINS

CAPILLARIES

The rate of breathing is about 15 to 20 per minute, but gets much faster when more oxygen is needed by the cells of the body during exercise, such as swimming or running.

The heart is a pump divided into two parts. One part pumps blood to the lungs and the other pumps it through the rest of the body. The tubes which take blood from the heart are the arteries. The blood returns to the heart through the veins. The arteries divide and subdivide, getting smaller and smaller, finishing as very small tubes called capillaries. It is from these capillaries that the oxygen passes from the blood to the body cells and it is here also that the blood receives the carbon dioxide from the same cells. The blood then passes from the capillaries via the veins back to the heart.

A similar process takes place when blood is pumped to the lungs.

THE EXPIRED AIR METHOD

It has been shown conclusively that this is the only really efficient method.

When a casualty has stopped breathing it is more important to get oxygen (air) into the lungs than to try to discover exactly why he has stopped breathing, although the cause is often obvious from the surroundings, etc., e.g. electrocution, coal-gas poisoning. One indication that breathing has stopped is discoloration of the lips, nails, ears and cheeks.

The air breathed out contains more than enough oxygen to supply the need of the casualty.

(1) If possible, lie casualty on back with head a little higher than feet.

(2) Tilt the casualty's head back and lift the jaw. This should move the tongue away from the back of the throat, the most common cause of respiratory obstruction.

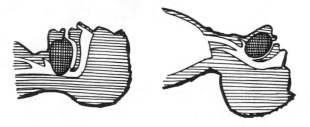

One of **three** things may now happen:

(i) Normal breathing may begin at once and consciousness may quickly return. The casualty's colour becomes pink again. He should be watched carefully in case he stops breathing again.

(ii) Normal breathing may begin but consciousness **not** return. Place in the coma position and keep the airway clear (see Aftercare, page 69). The victim may have bumped his head.

(iii) Breathing may return but be **noisy** which means that the airway is not fully clear. **All noisy breathing is obstructed breathing** (but there is no noise when the airway is completely blocked). Try to clear the airway fully; there may be some fluid in the throat.

(3) If breathing does not restart clean the mouth and throat of any obvious blockage by fluid, vomit, weed or other obstruction.

(4) If after clearing the throat there is still no sign of breathing:

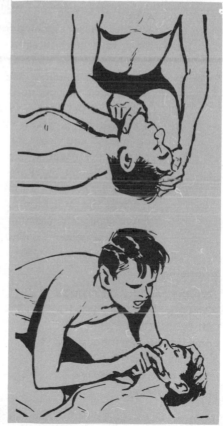

(i) Check that the head is still tilted back;

(ii) Take a deep breath;

(iii) Close his mouth and blow firmly but gently into his nose

or

Pinch his nose and blow firmly but gently into his mouth. As you do this the chest will **rise**.

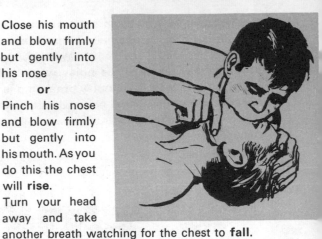

(iv) Turn your head away and take another breath watching for the chest to **fall**.

(v) Give four quick breaths and then continue with one breath every five seconds — 12 times a minute.

(vi) If the chest does not rise and fall you are not making a proper seal over his nose or mouth, or the airway is still obstructed and needs to be cleared again.

(vii) If the casualty is a baby make a seal with your mouth over his mouth **and** nose and breathe into him gently with a puff of the cheeks. Repeat this about 20–25 times a minute. Do not blow violently into a baby's lungs.

(viii) If the airway is clear it will not be long before the "pink" colour replaces the "blue" look. As consciousness returns the victim will start to breathe on his own; this is the time to stop resuscitation. Continue to hold his chin up and so keep his airway clear.

Vomiting

Turn the casualty on his side away from you and clear his mouth and throat with your finger. Then return the casualty onto his back and restart resuscitation if necessary.

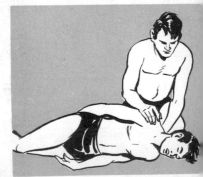

Air in Stomach

If the airway is only partially cleared, air may enter the stomach. This can usually be seen as a swelling of the upper part of the stomach. Gentle pressure will push the air out quite safely. If this should make the casualty sick start again to clear the airway before continuing resuscitation.

Drowning Accidents

Many casualties of drowning accidents do not have water in their lungs because the vocal chords at the entrance to the windpipe come together and the special flap prevents water entering the lungs.
If water does get into the lungs it cannot be removed, so do not waste time trying to do so; start resuscitation at once.
Fresh water in the lungs is absorbed very quickly into the blood stream; this dilutes the blood and affects the heart rapidly. In fresh water drowning **seconds count** so begin resuscitation **WITHOUT DELAY.** Salt water is not absorbed at all so the heart is not affected quite so rapidly, but again DO NOT DELAY resuscitation.

Demonstrating and Practising Expired Air Resuscitation

(1)   Practise breathing deeply in and out at five-second intervals.
(2)   Learn to put the head in the right position by practising with a partner. Close his mouth and support his jaw by placing your thumb and forefinger respectively down either side of his jaw bone; curl your other fingers and fit the knuckle of your second finger under his jaw. Make sure that your curled fingers do not press on the throat.
(3)   Get used to adopting the correct position for the operator by kneeling close beside your partner.
(4)   Take every chance of practising on a training mannikin or mask.

(5) For practice and demonstration purposes where a training aid is not available, lean over your partner and breathe down past his far cheek.

(6) Practise turning your partner from his front to his back to position him for resuscitation. Kneel by his side, stretch out the arm nearest to you and grasp his far shoulder with one hand and his hip with the other, at the same time clamping his wrist. With a steady pull with both arms, roll him over against your thighs. Lower him gently to the ground, supporting his head and shoulders as you do so. Then replace the other arm by his side.

Note: The techniques of Silvester Brosch and External Cardiac Compression and the related advanced physiology can be found in the Royal Life Saving Society *Resuscitation Handbook*.

Expired Air Resuscitation — Techniques in Water

In each case use the mouth to nose method. Close the subject's mouth and support his jaw in the normal manner for mouth-to-nose resuscitation, using that hand to extend the head; **and**

Standing in Shallow Water

support the subject's trunk either between his shoulder blades or under his far armpit with your other hand;

Or

Supported in Deep Water

support the subject with your other arm behind his neck with your hand gripping the bar or side.

Note: For practice and demonstration purposes for the above techniques, breathe beyond the subject's far cheek.

Or

Swimming in Deep Water

support the subject with your free hand under the back of his head.

Keep his face out of the water and avoid twisting his head. Keep the subject moving slowly with his body in the normal towing position.

Note: For practice and demonstration purposes the rescuer's mouth should be applied to the subject's forehead.

AFTERCARE AND ACTION IN SPECIAL CASES

AFTERCARE

Following resuscitation every recovered casualty should be taken immediately, and by ambulance if possible, to hospital or to a doctor for a check to make sure that all is well.

1. The Unconscious Casualty

An unconscious casualty who is breathing should be placed in the "coma position" (coma is the medical term meaning unconsciousness

from which a person cannot be woken, and so it differs from ordinary sleep). Keep the casualty in the coma position during transportation to hospital. Keep the airway clear by tilting the head back and holding the jaw forward. Restart resuscitation if necessary.

2. Severe External Bleeding

In extreme cases, bleeding may have to be stopped before commencing resuscitation, but do not delay resuscitation longer than absolutely necessary.

The most effective way to stop bleeding is by direct pressure with the fingers or hand over the bleeding site. A pad and bandage can replace this later. Move the casualty to hospital as soon as possible.

3. Shock

A dangerous state of physical collapse. There is always some degree of shock after all but the most minor injury and it is made worse by cold, lack of oxygen, loss of blood, pain and fear. A person who is shocked appears pale and the skin is cold and moist. The pulse will be weak and fast and the breathing shallow.

What to do:
Comfort and reassure.
Do not move the casualty more than is necessary: handle gently.
Lay casualty down with legs raised if possible: loosen tight clothing around neck, chest and waist.
Stop any bleeding.
Protect by covering with a coat, blankets, etc. under as well as over casualty's body.
Do not give anything to eat or drink.
Do not warm either by massage or by any other kind of artificial heat.
Send for medical help or ambulance as soon as possible.

4. Effect of Cold

Cold may lead to deterioration in the casualty's general condition. If cold but dry, wrap in a coat or blanket to prevent further heat loss.

If wet and cold and unclothed, the casualty should be dried quickly, then wrapped.

If wet and cold but fully clothed, the casualty should be wrapped in a dry blanket or coat.

Do not apply artificial heat; get to hospital as soon as possible.

5. Cramp

A constant painful contraction of the muscles. If it occurs in the muscles of a limb they should be stretched by straightening the limb and warmed by rubbing. If the muscles of back or stomach are involved, warm by vigorous rubbing.

Note: For comprehensive notes, see *First Aid*, published by St. John Ambulance Association, St. Andrew's Ambulance Association and The British Red Cross Society.

ACTION IN SPECIAL CASES

Electric Shock

Act quickly but be sure the casualty is not still connected to the current, or you may be another victim.

(a) Switch off current, remove electric plug or wrench cable free.

(b) If this is not possible, try to break contact by knocking or pulling casualty clear either by his clothes (taking care not to touch his bare skin), or with something which is dry and will not conduct electricity, e.g. wood, folded newspaper, heavy book, rubber, rope, etc. Do not, of course, use metal.

(c) When you do this stand on a dry surface. Be especially careful if there is any wetness about.

(d) If breathing has stopped, start resuscitation at once.

Manufactured Town Gas or Car Exhaust Poisoning

Do **not** use a naked light in the presence of gas.

The casualty may have a pink or reddish flush.

(a) Remove the casualty into fresh air.

(b) Start resuscitation as soon as you are clear of the contaminated air.

(c) Draw well clear between breaths to avoid contamination from casualty's exhaled air. **N.B.** The only gas present if you do not remain in the contaminated area is that in the casualty's lungs. So if you make sure you take a breath of clean air each time you will not be overcome by the gas in the casualty's lungs.

HINTS TO TEACHERS

General

It is desirable that all those teaching life saving should hold a recognised teaching qualification, such as A.S.A., S.T.A. or an academic qualification.

The R.L.S.S. Teacher's Certificate and Advanced Teacher's Certificate are designed to qualify those who do not hold any such recognised teaching qualifications, and the hints in this section are specially provided for them.

Those who already hold recognised teaching qualifications may feel it worthwhile to take these additional specific qualifications.

You as a Teacher

You should know your subject thoroughly; your mind should be clear and orderly; you must apply imagination to your lessons and stimulate the enthusiasm of the class. It is your approach which will sustain and develop the interest of the students. The safety of the class is your responsibility; ensure there is adequate supervision.

The Class

Class organisation will depend on:

- (a) pool time — most valuable, should be used for maximum practice in the water;
- (b) time and facilities for non-water activities (resuscitation, practice assessment of emergency situations);
- (c) the number of students, who should be divided into groups according to comparative ability and experience. Be prepared to move quick learners into a more advanced group when necessary;
- (d) the number of assistants available.

Pre-Session Demonstration

Before starting a series of lessons, it is desirable to organise a demonstration for the students of the full sequence of life-saving skills — from "reach, throw, etc" to "swimming rescue" (including landings and resuscitation) by a pair of competent qualified life savers. The Society's films are a useful prelude. (See note on page 78.)

The Students

Students need to be given:

    (a)   facts to memorise;

    (b)   skills to learn and practise.

They must be taught to assess what is required in an emergency and to choose and apply the appropriate skills.

Their powers of absorption will differ with each individual.

To help them — try to be **brief** — **clear** — **humorous**.

                     — give the "quick ones" plenty to do;

                     — give the "slow ones" more encouragement and attention.

In order to learn life-saving skills, students must be reasonably good swimmers — able to swim:

    (a)   100 yards fairly strongly by any stroke, other than back stroke;

    (b)   100 yards back stroke without the use of arms.

Variety of Approach in the Lesson

Lectures. Discussions. Demonstrations. Practical activities. Staged incidents. Training aids. Use of films, slides, strips, diagrams, illustrations.

Concentrate on **visual instruction**. It has more impact than the spoken word.

Structure of the Lesson

You must plan each lesson in advance. Written preparation helps to clarify ideas and ensure an orderly approach.

The class must have a clear understanding of the work to be done in each lesson. Outline the scope at the start. Summarise at the end.

In practical work aim at:

    (a)   clear demonstration;

    (b)   maximum practise by students;

(c) correction of faults;

(d) link with skills already learned.

In lectures:

(a) select specific subject material;

(b) break down into headings;

(c) keep it simple;

(d) do not attempt too much;

(e) emphasise the main points;

(f) check by regular questioning that students have understood.

Suggestions for Basic Instruction

Basic instruction will necessarily have to be adapted to the varying conditions and facilities available.

If possible, working groups of eight to ten students are most convenient. Instruct one group in one area, while another practises in another area. In early stages practice is best carried out where the water is of at least shoulder depth. Alternate groups at regular 3 to 4 minute intervals to prevent:

(a) boredom for some slow learners;

(b) students becoming chilled if listening or watching too long at a time.

While teaching:

(a) check swimming strokes;

(b) test endurance;

(c) check techniques previously learned;

(d) teach techniques required for the award in view;

(e) do not confine teaching to the syllabus of the particular award;

(f) include staged incidents and tests designed to stimulate adaptability.

Additional Reading

A.S.A. — *Swimming Instruction*. Sections on teaching and hygiene. Department of Education and Science — *Moving and Growing*. Chapter 3: Ways of Learning.

Syllabus of Skills

For water-work lessons, select skills from the following syllabus relevant to the stage of training and in enough variety to ensure interest.

Reach — Throw — Wade

Practise on land (hall); then, where pool time permits, in water.

Entries

From the side
   (a) straddle jump;
   (b) shallow dive.

From 3 to 4 feet
   (a) compact jump;
   (b) shallow dive.

Increase later up to 8 feet (where possible).

Tread Water

   (a) legs and arms;
   (b) legs only;
   (c) arms only.

Scull

Head first: 10 yards.
Feet first: 10 yards.

Recovery of Object

Open eyes under water.
Swim to the bottom — maximum 5 feet at first.
Swim and surface dive — head-first entry.
Swim and surface dive — feet-first entry.
Surface dive — recover object.
Swim back with it and land it.
Swim a length on the back supporting a heavier object.

Side Stroke and Life Saving Back Stroke

Practise in stages: one width — one length — 100 yards

Tows

Tow the subject by the Extended tow, by chin, hair and clothes.

Practise each in stages over 10, 20, 30 yards, using both side and life saving back strokes.

Repeat, using:

(a) "Chin tow".
(b) "Chin tow" with shoulder and breathing restraints.
(c) "Cross chest tow".
(d) "Cross chest tow" with restraint.

Helping the Subject to Land

At shallow end, after a 10-yard tow, help the subject to place his hands on the side.

Repeat: then land using Stirrup method.

Repeat as far as side: climb out with hand on top of the subject's hands. Help him out.

Approach

Swim to a co-operative subject. Speak to calm him and give loud, clear, brief instructions. Swim around behind the subject. Swim 10 yards, assisting the subject to swim to side.

Swim towards a struggling subject — "stand off" at a safe distance to avoid clutch. Tread water. Speak to calm.

Repeat, adding defensive action. Swim round behind the subject, keeping at a safe distance.

Repeat, taking a support for the subject to grasp. Speak to calm him. Instruct him what to do.

Repeat, adding tow with the support or towing aid.

Defensive Methods

Approach subject and "reverse".

Approach side of bath. Apply single leg block.

Approach subject; apply leg block.

Approach subject; apply leg block and counter.

Approach subject and "duck away".

76

Releases

Push-away break (from front neck or pinion hold).
Pull control (from wrist grip).
Arm pull (from wrist grip).
Elbow break (from back neck or pinion hold).
Joint pressure break (from pinned elbows).
Practise all with subjects who will apply a strong, determined clutch.

Resuscitation

Practise:

(a) in shallow water, supporting subject while standing at chest depth.

(b) in deep water, with subject supported against the side;

(c) for advanced students, while swimming in deep water.

Application of Skills

Having learned the skills, the students must be taught to apply them in different rescue sequences.

Brief subjects on their action. Three or four pairs can practise at one time depending on the space available.

Get the students to practise the approach and subsequent action for the following:

(1) An unconscious subject.

(2) A subject in a panic (a non-swimmer, a swimmer with cramp, etc).

(3) A subject who is unconscious, then after a distance regains consciousness, panics and struggles.

(4) A subject who is struggling, then after a distance becomes unconscious and stops breathing.

(5) Varied situations where the subject's action is unrevealed.

Criticise each rescue, pointing out how incorrect action has led to difficulty and even danger.

Assessment of Emergency Situations

Students must be given plenty of practice in relating their knowledge to typical theoretical emergencies in open water since these ass ss-ments are now a part of the examination conditions and specially introduced to help bridge the gap between swimming pool conditions and those of open water.

Such practice incidents can be done on blackboard or model: in the tests the examiner will pose the situation verbally, using a sketch or diagram.

In a club it may be possible to plan a session outdoors using suitable open water. This will give better value in interest and variety.

Note — Instructional Film

Explorer Films have produced an instructional film (16 mm.) in colour and details can be obtained from 58 Stratford Road, Bromsgrove, Worcs.

THE PROFICIENCY AWARDS

The proficiency awards enable those interested in water safety and life saving to measure their skill and progress. This section sets out:—

    a summary of the awards;
    general conditions for examinations;
    particular conditions of each examination.

Proficiency award holders are warned that conditions in open water may differ greatly from those in a swimming pool.

The examinations are summarised below in groups, in ascending order of importance in each group.

Safety Awards

Water Safety Award — for inexperienced or non-swimmers; to test knowledge of the rules of water safety applicable to inexperienced and non-swimmers, the ability to give simple basic help and elementary resuscitation.

Preliminary Safety Award ⎤ to test swimming competence and pre-
Advanced Safety Award ⎦ paratory life-saving skills.

Resuscitation

All awards require a knowledge of resuscitation but there are separate resuscitation tests as a general contribution to first-aid training.

Preliminary Resuscitation Award — elementary knowledge of expired air resuscitation.

Advanced Resuscitation Award — a standard test for first aid. (The details of this award are given in the R.L.S.S. Resuscitation Handbook. There is a Re-Examination test.)

Life Saving

Elementary Award — a general introduction to life saving.
Intermediate Award — a preparatory stage to the Bronze Medallion.
Bronze Medallion — the basic test of a qualified life saver.

Sub-Aqua Bronze Medallion — an adaptation of the Bronze Medallion test for members of underwater swimming clubs.

Bronze Cross
Award of Merit $\Big\}$ tests of greater stamina and knowledge.

Distinction Award — the highest practical test.

Diploma of the Society — a high standard of practical work and theory.

For repeat tests of the Bronze Medallion, Bronze Cross and Award of Merit, bars are awarded. For a repeat test of the Distinction Award a certificate is awarded.

Teaching

Teacher's Certificate — ability to teach to Bronze Cross level.

Advanced Teacher's Certificate — ability to teach to Diploma level.

Life Guard Corps

Life Guard Corps Members Proficiency Test — a test of life guard skills; bars (repeat tests) may be taken (details are in the Life Guard Corps Pamphlet).

GENERAL CONDITIONS FOR EXAMINATIONS

Membership

Candidates for the Society's proficiency awards must be individual members of the Society, or members of the body affiliated to the United Kingdom National Branch or one of its Branches, unless covered by one or more of the following exemptions:

  (a) candidates for the Safety Awards; the Elementary Award; and the Resuscitation Awards;

  (b) members of Her Majesty's Armed Forces;

  (c) candidates taking examinations in direct connection with the Duke of Edinburgh's Award Scheme.

Application for Examination

Application for examination should be made:

(a) Within a Branch area, to the Honorary Secretary of the Branch or Branch nominees (e.g., Branch Honorary Representatives);

(b) outside a Branch area, to the local Honorary Representative of the Society. When names are not known application should be made direct to the Secretary at Headquarters.

Application for examination should state:

the award(s) for which examination is required;

whether the appropriate examination forms are held;

the number of candidates to be presented;

the proposed place of examination;

alternative dates and times.

A minimum of fourteen days notice should be given. While the Society makes every endeavour to suit the convenience of candidates, it relies entirely on the support of voluntary Examiners and cannot guarantee always to accept the arrangements proposed.

Place of Examination

If the examination is to be conducted in a public swimming bath, responsibility for obtaining the agreement of the Bath Manager rests with the class instructor or, in the case of a single candidate, with the candidate himself.

Examinations may be taken in suitable open water.

Examiners

Examinations for the Society's awards may be conducted only by appointed Examiners of the Society, and no such Examiner may examine a candidate with whose instruction he has been directly concerned. The National Executive will, if necessary, modify this rule to meet particular circumstances which arise from time to time in overseas territories forming part of the United Kingdom National Branch, provided that written application is made to the Secretary at Headquarters before the examination is arranged.

While it is not the intention to interfere with any arrangement which has been adopted and worked well in the past, the National Executive reserves the right to refuse acceptance of any examination which has not been arranged in accordance with the above rules.

Examination Fees Payable

Examination fees, which may be altered by the National Executive from time to time, are payable by candidates as follows:

Test	Fee	Award
Water Safety Award	3s. 0d.	Metal lapel badge
Preliminary Safety Award	4s. 0d.	Metal lapel badge
Advanced Safety Award	5s. 0d.	Metal lapel badge
Preliminary Resuscitation Award	3s. 0d.	Metal lapel badge
Advanced Resuscitation Award	5s. 0d.	Metal lapel badge
Re-Examination	3s. 0d.	Certificate
Elementary Award	3s. 0d.	Costume Badge
Intermediate Award	4s. 0d.	Costume Badge
Bronze Medallion	6s. 0d.	Engraved Medallion
First bar	6s. 0d.	Clasp and Bar
Subsequent bars	5s. 0d.	Bar
Bronze Cross	6s. 0d.	Engraved Medallion
First bar	6s. 0d.	Clasp and Bar
Subsequent bars	5s. 0d.	Bar
Award of Merit	12s. 6d.	Engraved Medallion Costume Badge
First bar	6s. 0d.	Clasp and Bar
Subsequent bars	5s. 0d.	Bar
Distinction Award	17s. 6d.	Certificate Costume Badge
Repeat tests	10s. 0d.	Certificate
Diploma of the Society	£3 3s. 0d.	Certificate Costume Badge
Teacher's Certificate	7s. 6d.	Certificate
Advanced Teacher's Certificate	£1 0s. 0d.	Certificate Costume Badge
Life Guard Proficiency Test	5s. 0d.	Costume Badge
Repeat tests	5s. 0d.	Bar

A costume badge or pin badge (according to the type of award) may be purchased at extra cost by the successful candidate. For price list see page 142.

Forfeit of Examination Fees

Candidates who fail in an examination will forfeit their examination fees. Instructors are advised not to present candidates for examination until they are well up to the standard required.

Examination Forms

Before the start of the examination the appropriate examination forms, completed in all required details in duplicate (unless Branches indicate specifically that only one copy is wanted) and with the **surnames** of all candidates written in **block letters**, must be handed to the Examiner. The examination forms are the sole basis for the correct recording and issue of awards. Mistakes in details and illegible writing will result in errors and delay in the receipt of the awards.

Age Limit

In examinations for which there is an age limit, Examiners may at their discretion require proof of a candidate's age to be forwarded with the examination form. Such proof should take the form of a statement signed by a responsible person.

Conduct of Examinations

Examinations will be conducted in accordance with the *current* edition of the Handbook. The *sections* of each examination may be taken in any order to suit local requirements. But in the water test section the individual tests must be taken in the order given.

The primary requirement in the examinations is for the candidate to prove his ability in the Society's methods of life saving and resuscitation: a candidate who shows an acceptable standard of life-saving proficiency and speed will not be failed solely on imperfection of swimming strokes or diving technique. Candidates are not permitted to refer to the Handbook or other aids to memory during examination, nor are they allowed any artificial aid to swimming.

Back stroke will not be allowed in the approach swim, as it is difficult to keep the subject in sight. In any approach swim the last 5 yards must be head up, watching the subject.

Safety of Candidates

When a class of candidates is under examination the class instructor will be responsible for taking action if a candidate gets into difficulty due to exhaustion or other cause. The decision whether the candidate shall subsequently be permitted to continue the examination will rest with the Examiner after consultation with the Instructor. With the above exception the Examiner shall be solely responsible for the conduct of the examination.

Demonstration on Land

An Examiner may require a candidate to demonstrate a method on land if he is not satisfied with the candidate's performance of the method in the water.

Split Examinations

In schools and other particular cases in which it is impossible to conduct the whole examination of a class of candidates in one session, the oral tests and the practical demonstration of resuscitation may be separated from the water work by agreement with the Examiner provided that all candidates are ready to take the full examination before commencing any part of it. Only in very exceptional cases should this period exceed fourteen days.

If an examination is split the same Examiner should, if possible, conduct both sessions.

A large class of candidates may be split into sections, each section having a different Examiner.

Rest Period

No rest periods are specifically allowed for but the conduct of the test will normally allow short rest intervals. In the case of a single candidate, the Examiner will use his discretion.

Expired Air Resuscitation

In the examinations the method may be demonstrated with or without training aids.

This method is now accepted almost universally. If, however, a candidate produces a certificate from his religious leader that the method would not be allowed on religious grounds to save life in an emergency, he may be examined in the Silvester Brosch method instead. The certificate will be attached to the examination form.

Subjects

For all examinations the candidate and the subject should be of similar height and weight. Subjects will be briefed by the Examiner on any action required during the test.

Recovery of an Object

If the minimum depth of water available is greater than the depth laid down for the recovery of an object, or if the water conditions preclude the sighting of an object on the bottom with reasonable ease, the Examiner should satisfy himself that the candidate can execute a surface dive or swim down, without requiring the actual recovery of an object from the bottom.

If the candidate fails at his first attempt, the test must be repeated twice, both successfully.

Landing

Conditions in some swimming baths or unacceptable risk of injury to the subject may make it undesirable to carry out the actual landing. In these circumstances the candidate should be required to demonstrate the method without making the actual landing or, if necessary, to describe how it would be done.

Clothing

In examinations in which other clothes are required to be worn in addition to swimwear, such clothing must be of an ordinary everyday character and must be clean. The Examiner at his discretion, or at the request of the Bath Manager when the examination is being held in a public swimming bath, will refuse examination if the clothes worn by the candidate or subject are unsatisfactory in any respect.

Warning: Because of the increasing use of man-made fibres in the material used for clothing, nylon shirts and similar garments will **not** be removed over the head. Buttons on wet garments made of nylon type fabrics often become difficult to undo; if in these circumstances an attempt is made to remove the garment over the head with a neck opening which is too small, it is apt to become wrapped round the wearer's head and to obstruct his breathing. If the shirt or other garment worn cannot be completely unbuttoned down the front, and must therefore be removed over the head, it must be made of some natural fibre material, such as cotton.

Clothing Worn Overseas

The clothing specified in the various examination conditions consists of articles which are normally worn in the United Kingdom. In examinations conducted outside the United Kingdom Examiners have authority to substitute alternative items of clothing appropriate to local conditions, provided that the conditions of the tests are not thereby made easier.

Collusion Between Subject and Candidate

The subject is not permitted to give the candidate any assistance beyond carrying out instructions given to him verbally by the candidate. Collusion between candidate and subject will entail failure of the candidate, and the subject if he is also a candidate in the examination.

Termination of an Examination

In practical examinations if the candidate fails a particular test he shall be given the option of carrying on with the examination despite his failure or of terminating the examination without completion of the remaining tests.

Signature of Examination Forms

On completion of the examination the Examiner will sign the examination forms and indicate the names of candidates who have failed by ruling their names through. The total number of passes and failures should be inserted by the Examiner in the appropriate space on the form.

Forwarding of Forms and Fees

Responsibility for ensuring that the completed examination forms are forwarded *without delay* to the Branch or National Headquarters as appropriate (see above) rests with the *Instructor* of a class or, in the case of an individual candidate, with the *candidate himself.* Except in those cases in which arrangements exist, or are made, for periodical block payments of fees, the appropriate fees must be sent with the examination forms. Delay in the despatch of awards will occur if this is not done.

Repeat Tests (Bars to Awards)

Repeat tests (bars) may be taken for the Bronze Medallion, Bronze Cross, Award of Merit, and Distinction (and also for the Advanced Resuscitation and Life Guard Corps Proficiency Awards). The repeat test conditions are the same as those for the award.

A minimum period of one year must elapse before the examination for the basic award and the taking of the examination for the first bar to that award. For the second and subsequent bars only one bar may be gained in each calendar year and there must be a minimum period of six months between consecutive successful examinations.

For example — a candidate who gains the Bronze Cross on 3rd March 1967 is permitted to take the examination for his first bar to that award at any time after 2nd March 1968, and does so on 15th May 1968. Although the minimum period of six months will elapse on 14th November 1968 he must wait to take the examination for his second bar to the Bronze Cross until 1st January 1969, because he is not allowed to gain two bars to the same award in the calendar year 1968.

This rule does *not* prevent an award holder from taking examinations for bars to two or three separate awards in the same calendar year or within six months of each other.

Approval of National Executive

Examination results and the granting of the appropriate proficiency awards are subject to confirmation by the National Executive. Any candidate for a proficiency award being dissatisfied with the conduct (*not the result*) of his examination may appeal. Such appeal must in the first instance be sent in writing to the Honorary Secretary of the appropriate Branch or to the Secretary at the National Headquarters.

Replacement Awards

For the Safety Awards, the Preliminary Resuscitation Award and the Elementary and Intermediate Awards the examination forms are retained at Branches or Headquarters for six months from the date of receipt to deal with cases of loss in the post, etc. before the award reaches the candidate. After six months replacements cannot be made.

For the Advanced Resuscitation Award, and the Bronze Medallion and above, the examination forms are retained at Headquarters as records for a period of five years. During this period awards can be replaced on payment of the appropriate fee, provided they can be traced. In case of dispute the Society's records will be taken as final in the absence of other concrete evidence to the contrary.

Requests for replacement awards should state:

(a)   the award;
(b)   full name *at the time of examination*;

(c)   the year and month in which the examination was taken;

(d)   the name of the club, school or class.

Payment of the fee should *not* be made with the initial application, but should await confirmation that the award has been traced, at which time the cost of replacement will be notified. Replacement awards will be of the current design.

Only in exceptional circumstances (and **not** for purposes of pay qualification) can searches be carried out prior to the five-year period.

WATER SAFETY AWARD

Object: to test knowledge of the rules of water safety applicable to inexperienced and non-swimmers, the ability to give simple basic help to someone in difficulty in the water and elementary resuscitation.

Award: a metal lapel badge.

Age limit: none.

Examiners: the examination shall be conducted by one Examiner.

Examination Syllabus

The examination will consist of three sections:

    (1)   water safety;
    (2)   elementary rescue;
    (3)   elementary resuscitation.

1. Water Safety

Show a knowledge of water safety for non-swimmers by answering questions from the rules summarised for ease of reference on the next page (including the advice to parents).

2. Elementary Rescue

Demonstrate on land two methods of reaching someone in difficulties in the water, using:

    (a)   a branch or length of wood;
    (b)   two articles of clothing tied together.

Demonstrate on land throwing to *within reach* of a stationary subject over a distance of 20 feet:

    (a)   an unweighted rope;
    (b)   a large inflated ring or similar object.

3. Elementary Resuscitation

Demonstrate the expired air method to the satisfaction of the Examiner.

Explain the position of the head and what to do if the patient vomits, and if air enters the stomach.

WATER SAFETY RULES

If you cannot swim — LEARN!

Don't play in forbidden or dangerous places such as:
  canal banks;
  gravel pits;
  river banks;
  ponds.

Remember
  Home-made rafts soon sink.
  Ice melts quickly and breaks.
  Only go boating with an adult, and wear a life jacket.
  Take heed of notice boards.
  Do not hang anything over notice boards.

TO BATHE SAFELY

Only do so with your parent's permission and in their sight. Never bathe alone. Do not go in water deeper than waist level. Never bathe just after a meal or when hungry. Only use air beds or rubber rings in a safe place like the paddling pool — otherwise there is danger of being carried into deep water. Don't fool about in or near water. Don't run on wet surrounds.

If you fall in
  Keep calm.
  Call for help.
  Float on your back.
  To attract attention wave one arm only.

If someone else falls in
  Look for something to help pull him out (stick, rope, scarf), lie down so that you will not be pulled in too.
  If you cannot reach him, tell him to float on his back or throw any floating object (rubber ring or ball) for him to hold on to, then **fetch help.**

Always observe these rules and when you are a good swimmer, also learn the water safety code (see page 16 or R.O.S.P.A. water safety code).

Disregard of these rules may endanger the rescuer as well as the person in difficulties.

PARENTS!

At home, fence in garden pools and keep toddlers away from water. Always supervise non-swimmers when near open water. Only allow them in water which you know to be safe and when you are present. Observe local rules and advice where and when to bathe-never when danger flags are flying. Choose the centre of a beach and if possible an area supervised by a life-guard. If you are a non-swimmer and you see someone in difficulties and no competent life saver is at hand, you can organise a human chain or use a boat if available. **Otherwise** take action as shown above.

THE SAFETY AWARDS

Object: to test swimming competence and preparatory life-saving skills.

Award: a metal lapel badge.

Age Limit: none.

Examiners: the examination shall be conducted by one Examiner.

Dress for Water Test:

Candidate:

Ladies and girls: a dress, or blouse and slacks; swimwear.

   Men and boys: trousers and shirt; swimwear.

Pyjamas with long trousers are an acceptable alternative for both males and females.

Special Conditions

In genuine cases of disability candidates may take modified tests:

   (i)   for the preliminary award, a minimum of four of the six water tests;

   (ii)   for the advanced award, a minimum of six of the eight tests.

Examination forms will be endorsed "Disabled Candidate" under "Date of examination".

Examination Syllabus

For both tests the examination will consist of two sections:

   (1)   resuscitation test;

   (2)   water test.

PRELIMINARY SAFETY AWARD

1. Resuscitation
Demonstrate the expired air method to the satisfaction of the Examiner.

2. Water Test
Carry out the following tests as a continuous sequence:
- (a) Enter water feet first and swim 50 yards.
- (b) Tread water for 1 minute.
- (c) In deep water remove all clothing except swimwear.
- (d) Surface dive in a depth of not less than 4 feet and use feet to push off the bottom.
- (e) Swim 200 yards by any stroke.
- (f) Scull head or feet first for 30 feet.

ADVANCED SAFETY AWARD

1. Resuscitation
Demonstrate the expired air method of resuscitation for at least one minute to the satisfaction of the Examiner.

2. Water Test
Carry out the following tests as a continuous sequence:
- (a) Enter the water feet first and tread water for 3 minutes (1 minute legs only, 2 minutes arms only).
- (b) Swim 100 yards in less than 4 minutes.
- (c) Recover an object (5 to 10 lbs) from a depth of 6 feet (or nearest depth available, but not less than 5 feet). Land the object.
- (d) In deep water remove all clothing except swimwear in less than 20 seconds.
- (e) Swim 200 yards on the back without use of arms or artificial aids.
- (f) Swim 200 yards freestyle, other than backstroke without arms.
- (g) Scull head first and feet first, each for 30 feet.
- (h) Leave deep water without the use of steps or assistance.

PRELIMINARY RESUSCITATION AWARD

Object: to test ability to perform the expired air method of resuscitation, and elementary knowledge of respiration and blood circulation.

Award: a metal lapel badge.

Age Limit: none.

Examiners: the examination shall be conducted by one Examiner.

Examination Syllabus

The examination will consist of two sections:

(1) demonstration of the expired air method of resuscitation;
(2) oral test.

1. Demonstration

(a) Demonstrate to the satisfaction of the examiner the correct positioning of the subject and the mouth-to-nose technique of the expired air method.

(b) Demonstrate the action to be taken in case of:

   (i) vomit;
   (ii) air entering the stomach;
   (iii) recovery, placing the subject in the coma position.

2. Oral Test

(a) Answer questions on the elementary principles of respiration and blood circulation and the reasons for the positioning of the subject in the expired air method.

(b) Explain the use of the three techniques for carrying out the expired air method.

ELEMENTARY

ELEMENTARY AWARD

Object: to test the ability of the competent young swimmer in life saving at introductory level and to encourage further training. The holder is **not** qualified to attempt a rescue in deep water.

Award: a costume badge.

Age Limit: none.

Examiners: the examination shall be conducted by one Examiner.

Dress for Water Test:
Candidate and subject: swimwear.

Examination Syllabus

The examination will consist of three sections:

- (1) resuscitation test;
- (2) water test;
- (3) questions on water safety.

1. Resuscitation

Demonstrate the expired air method for a period of not less than 3 or more than 6 minutes, at the Examiner's discretion, to show:

- (a) the mouth-to-nose method;
- (b) the mouth-to-mouth method;
- (c) the action for vomit;
- (d) the coma position.

2. Water Test

(a) Enter the water, swim 25 yards to the subject.
Tow for 25 yards by any approved method selected by the candidate. On completion of the tow secure the subject in the support position.

(b) Jump or dive into the water, surface and swim 10 yards. Recover an object (5 to 10 lbs) from a depth of at least 4 feet. Bring to the starting point using life saving backstroke.

3. Water Safety

Answer four questions on water safety.

INTERMEDIATE AWARD

Object: to test the ability of the more competent swimmer at a stage preparatory to the Bronze Medallion. The holder is **not** qualified to attempt a contact rescue in deep water.

Award: a costume badge.

Age limit: none.

Examiners: the examination shall be conducted by one Examiner.

Dress for Water Test:
Candidate and subject: swimwear.

Examination Syllabus

The examination will consist of three sections:

    (1)   resuscitation test;
    (2)   water test;
    (3)   questions on water safety.

1. Resuscitation

Demonstrate the expired air method for a period of not less than 3 or more than 6 minutes, at the Examiner's discretion, to show:

    (a)   the mouth-to-nose method;
    (b)   the mouth-to-mouth method;
    (c)   the action for vomit;
    (d)   the coma position.

2. Water Test

    (a)   Enter the water, swim 50 yards to the subject and demonstrate "the Reverse": then approach the subject from behind.
           Tow for 50 yards by any approved method selected by the candidate.
           Land the subject by the Stirrup method.

(b)   Enter shallow water with a straddle jump, swim 20 yards to a subject considered to be unconscious and not breathing.

Tow by any approved method selected by the candidate to water shallow enough to stand in.

Demonstrate mouth-to-nose resuscitation while walking the subject to the side: then secure him in the support position.

(c)   Jump or dive into the water, surface and swim 10 yards. Recover an object (5 to 10 lbs) from a depth of at least 5 feet. Bring to the starting point using life saving backstroke.

3. Water Safety

Answer four questions on water safety.

BRONZE MEDALLION

Object: this is the basic test of a qualified life saver, who must show ability to carry out an effective rescue over a reasonable distance.

Award: an engraved bronze medallion.

Age Limit: 13 or over.

Examiners: the examination shall be conducted by one Examiner.

Dress for Water Test:
  Candidate: swimwear, except in test 2(a), when the following additional clothing will be worn:
    Ladies: blouse, skirt or slacks.
    Men: long-sleeved shirt, trousers.
  Pyjamas with long trousers are an acceptable alternative for ladies and men.
  Subject: swimwear.

Examination Syllabus

The examination will consist of three sections:

  (1)   resuscitation test;
  (2)   water test;
  (3)   assessment of action in an emergency situation.

1. Resuscitation

  (a)   Demonstrate the expired air method for a period of not less than 3 or more than 6 minutes, at the Examiner's discretion, to show:

      (i)   the mouth-to-nose method;
      (ii) the mouth-to-mouth method;

(iii) the action for vomit.

Following each, explain the techniques involved.

(b) Answer two questions on respiration and blood circulation.

2. Water Test

(a) Enter shallow water as for unknown conditions, swim 20 yards to the subject.

Tow to the starting point by any approved method selected by the candidate. Land the subject by the Stirrup method.

(b) Enter deep water with a straddle jump, swim 50 yards to the subject and demonstrate "the Reverse": then approach the subject from behind.

Tow for 50 yards by the Chin tow: during the tow the candidate must show ability to control the subject, who will struggle vigorously twice.

On completion of the tow secure the subject in the support position.

(c) Enter deep water, swim 50 yards to the subject and demonstrate a defence action (other than "the Reverse") specified by the Examiner: then approach the subject from behind.

Tow for 50 yards by the Cross Chest tow: during the tow the candidate must show ability to control the subject, who will struggle vigorously once.

On completion of the tow secure the subject in the support position.

The time allowance for this test is $4\frac{1}{2}$ minutes.

(d) Enter shallow water, swim 10 yards to a subject considered to be unconscious and not breathing.

Tow by the Extended tow to the nearest point of support in deep water and demonstrate mouth-to-nose resuscitation for three cycles.

Continue the tow to water shallow enough to stand in and demonstrate mouth to nose resuscitation while walking the subject at least 5 yards to the side.

Unaided, land the subject, considered to be unconscious but breathing, by the straight arm method and place in the coma position.

(e)   Demonstrate in the water a release specified by the Examiner from each of the three types of clutch.
Take up any approved towing position after each release.

(f)   Jump or dive into the water, surface and swim 10 yards. Recover an object (5 to 10 lbs) from a depth of at least 6 feet. Bring to the starting point using life saving backstroke.

3. Assessment of an Emergency Situation

The Examiner will describe a typical open-water emergency. The candidate will be required to explain the action he would take.

SUB-AQUA BRONZE MEDALLION

Object: this is the life-saving test for a qualified Diver, who must show ability to carry out an effective rescue both with and without the assistance of diving gear.

Award: an engraved bronze medallion.

Pre-requisite: the candidate must be a member of an underwater swimming club.

Age Limit: 16 or over.

Examiners: the examination shall be conducted by a specially appointed Examiner.

Dress for Water Test:
Swimwear, unless specified otherwise.

Examination Syllabus

The examination will consist of four sections:

  (1) water test with diving gear;
  (2) water test without diving gear;
  (3) resuscitation test;
  (4) assessment of action in an emergency situation.

1. Water Test with Diving Gear

  (a) Both candidate and subject will be dressed in a wet suit, jacket and trousers (dry suit optional), life jacket of the inflatable type, charged-air cylinder demand valve, weight belt, and fins.

  These items should be in good condition and will be subject to inspection by the Examiner.

Both candidate and subject will be weighted for neutral buoyancy.

Enter deep water making a shallow forward entry and demonstrate neutral buoyancy.

Fin 50 yards to deep water, surface dive to the subject prepositioned on the bottom.

Remove his weight belt and bring him to the surface. Immediately inflate the subject's life jacket,* remove his mask and snorkel, lift your own mask.

Apply expired air resuscitation for four cycles.

Tow the subject at least 20 yards to shallow water, giving two breaths every 15 to 20 seconds during the tow.

In shallow water demonstrate expired air resuscitation while walking with the subject a distance of at least 5 yards to the side.

At this point explain to the Examiner how you would best use another competent life saver.

(b) Both candidate and subject will wear mask, fins and open-ended snorkel.

Enter as if for unknown water and fin using over arm strokes 50 yards to the subject.

Tow him continuously, 25 yards using B.S-A.C. method No. 2 and 25 yards using B.S-A.C. method No. 1.

In deep water remove the subject without assistance, and place in the coma position.

2. Water Test Without Diving Gear

(a) Enter deep water with a straddle jump, swim 50 yards to the subject and demonstrate "the Reverse": then approach the subject from behind.

Tow for 50 yards by the Chin tow: during the tow the candidate must show ability to control the subject, who will struggle vigorously twice.

On completion of the tow secure the subject in the support position.

* For the purpose of the examination the CO_2 inflation of the life jacket is not required. The candidate will be expected to raise his arm to indicate to the Examiner that he has carried out this operation, whereupon the subject may orally inflate his own life jacket. Air inflatable life jackets should be inflated by the rescuer.

(b) Enter shallow water, swim 10 yards to a subject considered to be unconscious and not breathing.

Tow by the Extended tow to the nearest point of support in deep water and demonstrate mouth to nose resuscitation for three cycles.

(c) Demonstrate in the water a release specified by the Examiner from each of the three types of clutch.

Take up any approved towing position after each release.

3. Resuscitation

(a) Demonstrate the expired air method for a period of not less than 3 or more than 6 minutes, at the Examiner's discretion, to show:

    (i)   the mouth-to-nose method;

    (ii) the mouth-to-mouth method;

    (iii) the action for vomit.

Following each explain the techniques involved.

(b) Answer two questions on respiration and blood circulation.

4. Assessment of an Emergency Situation

The Examiner will describe a typical open-water emergency. The candidate will be required to explain the action he would take.

BRONZE CROSS

Object: this is a test of a qualified life saver, who must show ability to carry out effective rescues over longer distances, and is a preparatory stage to the Award of Merit.

Award: an engraved bronze cross.

Pre-requisite Qualification: the Bronze Medallion.

Examiners: the examination shall be conducted by one Examiner.

Dress for Water Test:
Candidate; swimwear, except in test 2(a), when the following additional clothing will be worn:
Ladies: blouse, skirt or slacks.
Men, long-sleeved shirt, trousers
Pyjamas with long trousers are an acceptable alternative for ladies and men.

Subject: swimwear.

Examination Syllabus

The examination will consist of three sections:

(1) resuscitation test;
(2) water test;
(3) assessment of action in an emergency situation.

1. Resuscitation

Demonstrate the expired air method, with action for vomit, to the satisfaction of the Examiner.

2. Water Test

(a) Enter shallow water as for unknown conditions, swim 20 yards to the subject.

Tow to the starting point by any approved method selected by the candidate.

Land the subject by the Stirrup method.

(b) Enter deep water with a straddle jump, swim 75 yards to the subject and demonstrate "the Reverse": then approach the subject from behind.

Tow for 75 yards by the Chin tow: during the tow the candidate must show ability to control the subject, who will struggle vigorously twice.

On completion of the tow secure the subject in the support position.

(c) Enter deep water, swim 75 yards to the subject and demonstrate a defence action (other than "the Reverse") specified by the Examiner: then approach the subject from behind.

Tow for 75 yards by the Cross Chest tow: during the tow the candidate must show ability to control the subject, who will struggle vigorously once.

On completion of the tow secure the subject in the support position.

The time allowance for this test is $4\frac{1}{2}$ minutes.

(d) Enter shallow water, swim 10 yards to a subject considered to be unconscious and not breathing.

Tow by the Extended tow to the nearest point of support in deep water and demonstrate mouth to nose resuscitation for three cycles.

Continue the tow to water shallow enough to stand in and demonstrate mouth-to-nose resuscitation while walking the subject at least 5 yards to the side.

Unaided, land the subject, considered to be unconscious but breathing, by the straight arm method and place in the coma position.

(e) Demonstrate in the water a release specified by the Examiner from each of the three types of clutch.

Take up any approved towing position after each release.

(f) Jump or dive into the water, surface and swim 10 yards. Recover an object (5 to 10 lbs) from a depth of at least 6 feet. Bring to the starting point using life saving backstroke.

3. Assessment of an Emergency Situation

The Examiner will describe a typical open-water emergency. The candidate will be required to explain the action he would take.

AWARD OF MERIT

Object: this is an advanced test of a qualified life saver, who must show ability to carry out effective rescues of different types over longer distances. It forms a useful preparatory examination for the Life Guard Corps Members Proficiency Award.

Award: an engraved gilt medallion.

Pre-requisite Qualification: the Bronze Medallion.

Age Limit: 15 or over.

Examiners: the examination shall be conducted by one Grade 1 Examiner.

Dress for Water Test:
Candidate and subject; swimwear, except in tests 2(a) and (b), when the following additional clothing will be worn:
Ladies: blouse with long sleeves, skirt or slacks.
Men: long-sleeved shirt, trousers.

Examination Syllabus

The examination will consist of three sections:

(1) resuscitation test;
(2) water test;
(3) assessment of action in an emergency situation.

1. Resuscitation

(a) Demonstrate the Silvester Brosch method,* with action for vomit, for a period of not less than 3 or more than 6 minutes, at the Examiner's discretion.

---

* These techniques and the related physiology are contained in the *R.L.S.S. Resuscitation Handbook.*

(b) Demonstrate the expired air method, with action for vomit, to the satisfaction of the Examiner.

(c) Demonstrate ability in the diagnosis of cardiac arrest; demonstrate the technique of External Cardiac Compression* and explain the cycle of resuscitation combined with the expired air method.

Note: When demonstrating E.C.C. *on no account* must pressure be applied to a human body.

(d) Answer four questions on related physiology* and aftercare.

2. Water Test

(a) Enter shallow water feet first, swim 25 yards to the subject.

Tow to the starting point by the Cross Chest tow.

Unaided, land the subject by the straight arm method and place in the coma position.

The time allowance from the rescuer entering the water until he touches the side on his return is 2 minutes.

(b) In deep water remove all clothing except swimwear within 30 seconds.

(c) Enter deep water with a straddle jump, swim 75 yards to the subject.

Demonstrate a defence action specified by the Examiner: then approach the subject from behind.

Tow for 75 yards by any approved method selected by the candidate.

On completion of the tow secure the subject in the support position.

(d) Enter deep water with a shallow dive, swim 75 yards to a struggling subject. Approach from the front and effect a release from an unrevealed clutch.

Tow for 75 yards by the Chin tow: during the tow the candidate must show ability to control the subject, who will struggle vigorously twice.

On completion of the tow secure the subject in the support position.

(e) Make a shallow entry into deep water, swim 75 yards to a subject considered to be unconscious and not breathing.

---

* These techniques and the related physiology are contained in the *R.L.S.S. Resuscitation Handbook.*

Demonstrate deep-water resuscitation for three cycles.

Tow at least 20 yards to water shallow enough to stand in.

Demonstrate mouth-to-nose resuscitation while walking the subject at least 5 yards to the side.

Unaided, land the subject by the straight arm method and continue resuscitation.

After 10 cycles the subject is considered to have restarted breathing regularly but remains unconscious; treat for shock.

(f) Demonstrate in the water a release specified by the Examiner from each of the two types of clutch not already tested.

Following the second release tow the subject at least 10 yards to deep water (minimum 6 feet) and land unaided.

(g) Jump or dive into the water, surface and swim 10 yards. Recover two objects (each 5 to 10 lbs, placed at least 3 yards apart at a depth of at least 6 feet) before surfacing. Bring them to the starting point using life saving backstroke.

3. Assessment of an Emergency Situation

The Examiner will describe a typical open-water emergency. The candidate will be required to explain the action he would take.

DISTINCTION AWARD

Object: this is a more advanced test of a qualified life saver who must show all round practical ability of a high standard.

Award: an inscribed certificate and a costume badge.

Pre-requisite Qualification: the Award of Merit.

Age Limit: 16 or over.

Examiners: the examination shall be conducted by two Grade 1 Examiners.

Dress for Water Test:
 Candidate and subject: swimwear, except in tests 2(a) and (b), when the following additional clothing will be worn:
  Ladies: blouse with long sleeves, skirt or slacks.
  Men: long-sleeved shirt, trousers.

Examination Syllabus

The examination will consist of three sections:

 (1) resuscitation test;
 (2) water test;
 (3) assessment of action in an emergency situation.

1. Resuscitation

 (a) Demonstrate the Silvester Brosch method, with action for vomit, to the satisfaction of the Examiner.
 (b) Demonstrate the expired air method, with action for vomit, to the satisfaction of the Examiner.

(c)   Demonstrate ability in the diagnosis of cardiac arrest and demonstrate, on a recognised manikin or model, external cardiac compression combined with expired air resuscitation.

(d)   Answer four questions on related physiology and aftercare.

2. Water Test

(a)   Enter shallow water feet first, swim 25 yards to the subject.

Tow to the starting point by the Cross Chest tow.

Unaided land the subject by the straight arm method and place in the coma position.

The time allowance from the rescuer entering the water until he touches the side on his return is: men, $1\frac{1}{2}$ minutes; ladies, 2 minutes.

(b)   In deep water remove all clothing except swimwear within 30 seconds.

(c)   Enter deep water with a straddle jump, swim 100 yards to the subject.

Demonstrate a defence action specified by the Examiner: then approach the subject from behind.

Tow for 100 yards by any approved method selected by the candidate.

On completion of the tow secure the subject in the support position.

(d)   Enter deep water with a shallow dive, swim 100 yards to a struggling subject.

Approach from the front and effect a release from an unrevealed clutch.

Tow for 100 yards by the Chin tow: during the tow the candidate must show ability to control the subject, who will struggle vigorously twice.

On completion of the tow secure the subject in the support position.

(e)   Make a shallow entry into deep water, swim 75 yards to a subject considered to be unconscious and not breathing.

Demonstrate deep-water resuscitation for three cycles.

Tow for 75 yards: during the tow repeat resuscitation in deep water twice, each for three cycles.

On reaching water shallow enough to stand in continue resuscitation while walking the subject at least 5 yards to the side.

Unaided, land the subject by the straight arm method and continue resuscitation.

After 10 cycles the subject is considered to have restarted breathing regularly but remains unconscious; treat for shock.

(f) Demonstrate in the water a release specified by the Examiner from each of the two types of clutch not already tested.

Following the second release tow the subject at least 10 yards to deep water (minimum 6 feet) and land unaided.

(g) Jump or dive into the water, surface and swim 10 yards. Recover two objects (each 5 to 10 lbs, placed at least 5 yards apart, at a depth of at least 8 feet) before surfacing. Bring them to the starting point using life saving backstroke.

(h) Separate two swimmers locked together in deep water. Make a double tow for 20 yards to shallow water. Assist them from the water.

3. Assessment of an Emergency Situation

The Examiner will describe a typical open-water emergency. The candidate will be required to explain the action he would take.

THE DIPLOMA OF THE SOCIETY

Object: this is the highest award of the Society, designed to show a high standard in practical work and theory.

Award: an inscribed certificate and a costume badge;
additionally for a pass with honours: a gold medal.

Pre-requisite Qualification: the Award of Merit.

Age Limit: 17 or over at the time of the practical test.

Application: application for examination must be made in writing to the Honorary Secretary of the Branch or to the Secretary at Headquarters as appropriate. The application must include:
- (i)   the full name and address of the candidate;
- (ii) the date and place of examination for the Award of Merit;
- (iii) the examination fee of three guineas.

Conduct: the examination is conducted in two separate parts:
- (1) a practical test (as for the Distinction Award);
- (2) a written test.

Note: At the Commonwealth Conference, 1966, it was agreed that the Diploma should show the holder to be a first-class all-rounder in life-saving ability. The Commonwealth Technical Advisory Committee was asked to investigate the revision of the Diploma on the following basis: a candidate for the Diploma would qualify by holding

the Distinction Award to show practical ability;

an Advanced Instructor's Award;

a Grade 1 Examiner's card.

The Commonwealth Conference in 1971 will be asked to make a decision.

The United Kingdom National Branch has therefore made an anticipatory move by introducing the conditions of the Distinction Award as the Diploma practical test.

114

Special Conditions

(a)   The holding of the Distinction Award does **not** exempt the candidate from taking the practical test.

(b)   A candidate who fails the practical test is not eligible to take the written test.

(c)   The practical test must be taken not less than twenty-eight days or more than eight months before the written test except when the written test is taken a second time.

(d)   The candidate who fails the written test at the first attempt shall have the option of sitting for the next written test, without again taking the practical test, on payment of a further fee of two guineas and provided that notice of his intention to do so is given not less than twenty-eight days before the date of the next written test.

   Only in exceptional cases, such as illness, will candidates be permitted to postpone their written examination until the next occasion. In such cases the candidate should immediately inform the Branch or Headquarters as appropriate.

(e)   The written test will be held on a Saturday in May and October each year.

(f)   The Distinction Certificate (or Re-test Certificate) will be awarded to the candidate who passes the practical test (including a candidate who fails the written test).

(g)   The Diploma of the Society will be awarded to candidates who pass the practical test and obtain not less than 60 per cent of the maximum marks in the written test, and not less than 50 per cent for each question in the written test.

   The Diploma with Honours will be awarded to candidates who obtain a "pass with exceptional merit" in all sections of the practical test, and not less than 80 per cent for each question in the written examination.

The Practical Test

The conditions are the same as those for the Distinction Award (page 111). The Distinction Award examination form will be used endorsed "Diploma" in red after "Distinction Award" and when applicable "pass with exceptional merit in all sections" on the reverse with candidates' names and signed by both examiners.

The Written Test

Answer five of six questions based on the following syllabus:

(a) The importance of physical exercise on the growth and development of the body, with special reference to the effect of swimming.

(b) The importance and advantages of swimming to the individual and to the community.

(c) The fundamental physiology concerning the structure and functions of the lungs, the circulation of the blood and muscle nutrition.

(d) The effects of, and recuperation from, moderate and excessive exercise. The treatment of cramp.

(e) The causes of, and the steps to be taken to remedy, asphyxia (particularly electric shock, strangulation, carbon monoxide poisoning and drowning); shock, its action and treatment.

(f) Modern trends of thought in relation to life saving and resuscitation.

The time allowed for the examination will be 3 hours. Candidates may not refer to any books, papers on other aids to memory during the examination.

The time and place of the examination, and the appointment of invigilators will be arranged by the Branch or Headquarters as appropriate. The examination paper will be supplied from Headquarters in a sealed envelope which will be opened by the invigilator in the presence of the candidate(s) at the start of the examination.

A candidate who writes in a language other than English will be responsible for bearing the cost of subsequent translation which will be arranged by the Branch, local Honorary Representatives or Headquarters as appropriate, in which case both original and translation must be submitted. The candidate will not be permitted to arrange for the translation of his answers. Examination papers will be set only in the English language.

A list of reference books recommended for study and notes for the guidance of intending candidates can be obtained on application to the Honorary Branch Secretaries or to Headquarters.

TEACHER'S CERTIFICATE

Object: to qualify those wishing to teach life saving up to and including the Bronze Cross.

Award: a certificate.

Pre-requisite Qualification: the Bronze Medallion.

Age Limit: 16 or over.

Examiners: the examination shall be conducted by one Examiner.

Lectures: the candidate should attend, where possible, before taking the examination a course of lectures arranged by the Branch to cover the syllabus up to and including the Bronze Cross.

Class: the candidate must train and present a class of not less than four candidates for the Bronze Medallion.

Examination Syllabus

(1) Teach the class a life-saving skill selected by the Examiner.
(2) Instruct the class on;
    (a) expired air resuscitation;
    (b) a point, selected by the Examiner, on respiration and blood circulation.
(3) Present the class for the Bronze Medallion examination.
(4) Answer six questions covering the following:
    (a) class management and safety;
    (b) personal and pool hygiene;
    (c) general principles of water safety, life saving and the treatment of the apparently drowned.
(5) Demonstrate in the water three of the following as selected by the Examiner:
    (a) a defence skill;
    (b) a surface dive;
    (c) a tow;
    (d) breast, side or life saving back stroke;
    (e) a release.
Explain the common faults in the skills demonstrated and describe how they are corrected.

ADVANCED TEACHER'S CERTIFICATE

Object: to qualify those wishing to teach life saving up to and including the Diploma of the Society.

Award: a certificate and a costume badge.

Pre-requisites:

(a) the Teacher's Certificate,* and either the Award of Merit or the Advanced Resuscitation Award;

(b) the candidate must have presented at least twelve successful candidates for the Bronze Medallion.

Examiners: the examination shall be conducted by two specially appointed Grade 1 Examiners.

Lectures: the candidate should attend, where possible, before taking the examination a course of lectures arranged by the Branch to cover the syllabus up to and including the Diploma.

Examination Syllabus

(1) Instruct a class of not less than four persons on the techniques of:

    (a) Silvester Brosch;

    (b) External Cardiac Compression.

(2) Analyse the class's performance in the water of five water safety or life-saving skills selected by the Examiner.

Explain the common faults and describe how they are corrected.

(3) Teach the class the technique of expired air resuscitation in deep water.

(4) Answer four questions from *each* of the following:

    (a) related physiology;

    (b) after-care;

    (c) methods of relating life-saving training to emergency situations;

    (d) knowledge of training aids and their use.

* The former Instructor's Certificate is acceptable.

GENERAL

Administration Manual

A separate pamphlet on administration has been prepared, so that the size of the instructional handbook shall be as compact as possible. The administration manual contains the duties of Honorary Representatives and landmarks in the development of the Society, both formerly included in this Handbook.

THE COMMONWEALTH SOCIETY

Patron

Her Majesty The Queen is the fourth Sovereign to honour the Society as Patron.

Commonwealth Council

The Royal Life Saving Society is a Commonwealth organisation, governed by a Commonwealth Council, with five main National Branches — United Kingdom, Canada, Australia, New Zealand and Malaysia. R.L.S.S. Trinidad and Tobago and R.L.S.S. Jamaica are represented on the Council by the United Kingdom Members.

The Grand President is Admiral of the Fleet The Earl Mountbatten of Burma.

The Royal Life Saving Society — United Kingdom

The United Kingdom National Branch is responsible for co-ordinating the work of the Society in all parts of the Commonwealth lying outside the jurisdiction of the other National Branches, and consists of:

(a)   the Home Branches — the Branches in the United Kingdom and the Leinster, Munster and Connacht Branch.

(b)   the Home non-Branch areas — those areas in the United Kingdom lying outside the Branch areas, in which the work is co-ordinated by Honorary Representatives dealing direct with Headquarters.

(c)   the Overseas Branches — the Branches outside the United Kingdom which are represented on the Commonwealth Council by the United Kingdom Members of the Council.

(d)   the Overseas non-Branch areas — countries overseas in which the work is co-ordinated by Honorary Representatives who deal direct with the Headquarters.

The work of the United Kingdom National Branch is guided and co-ordinated by the National Executive under the general supervision of the United Kingdom Council and in accordance with the provisions of a Constitution approved by the Council.

The Headquarters of the United Kingdom National Branch are combined for ease of administration with the Headquarters of the Commonwealth Society in Desborough House, London.

It is the policy of the National Executive to strengthen the National Branch organisation by extending the number of home Branches to cover the non-branch areas as soon as possible and several new branches have been and are being formed. This increase in the number of branches has led to the creation of an extra tier in the organisation — the Region — and this system is currently under trial.

The "man on the spot" in both Branch and non-branch areas is the Honorary Representative. This is a very important appointment and the progress of the work of the Society depends very much on his or her enthusiasm, energy and intelligence.

The present development of the Society can best be illustrated by the diagram on the page opposite.

THE ROYAL LIFE SAVING SOCIETY
COMMONWEALTH COUNCIL

R.L.S.S. United Kingdom	R.L.S.S. Canada	R.L.S.S. Australia	R.L.S.S. New Zealand	R.L.S.S. Malaysia	R.L.S.S. Trinidad and Tobago	R.L.S.S. Jamaica

Fiji Branch

Branches	Non-branch areas	Overseas Branches	Overseas Representatives
Bristol		Gibraltar	Bahamas
Cambridge		Hong Kong	Bermuda
County of Sussex		Malta	Ceylon
Devon		Matabeleland	Cyprus
Essex		Rhodesia	Gambia
Gloucester		Singapore	Gilbert and Ellice
Guernsey		Zambia	Islands
Hertfordshire			H.M. Forces in
Huntingdon and			Germany
Peterborough			India
Kent			Kenya
Leeds and District			Nigeria
Leicester and			Pakistan
Rutland			St. Helena
Leinster, Munster			St. Lucia
and Connacht			Seychelles
Lincolnshire			Tanzania
Liverpool and			Uganda
District			
Manchester and			
District			
Middlesex			
Northamptonshire	Somerset		
North Lancashire	South Wales		
Northumberland	Staffordshire		
and Durham	Suffolk		
North Wales	Surrey		
North Yorkshire	Thames Valley		
Nottinghamshire	Ulster		
Scottish	Warwickshire		
Sheffield and	Wessex		
District	Worcestershire		

APPOINTMENT OF EXAMINERS

Lists

Examiners carry out their duties voluntarily in support of the Society's work and are appointed by Headquarters or the Branch Executive Committee who will keep up to date lists of names and addresses of appointments. The *Examiners Manual* gives guidance on their duties.

Grades

There are the following grades of examiners:

(a) Safety Award Examiners: authorised to examine:—
  Water Safety Proficiency Award;
  Preliminary Safety;
  Advanced Safety.

(b) Grade 2 Examiners: authorised to examine:—
  the above awards in (a);
  Elementary;
  Intermediate;
  Bronze Medallion;
  Bronze Cross;
  Teacher;
  Preliminary Resuscitation;
and by special appointment:
  Sub-Aqua Bronze Medallion.

(c) Grade 1 Examiners: authorised to examine:—
  the above awards in (a) and (b);
  Advanced Resuscitation;
  Award of Merit;
  Distinction;
and by special appointment
  Diploma;
  Advanced Teacher;
  Grade 1 and 2 Examiners;
  Life Guard Proficiency.

Branch Selection Panel

Each Branch Executive shall elect from amongst its Grade 1 Examiners a special panel whom it considers to be competent in every way to conduct examinations of candidate Examiners. Two members of such a panel shall be required to conduct an examination. (In the case of non-branch areas and overseas areas, Headquarters will be responsible for devising a suitable arrangement.)

General Qualifications

(a)   All Examiners must be aged 18 or over.
(b)   All candidates for Grade 2 Examiner must hold the Bronze Medallion.

Safety Award Examiners

For the appointment of Safety Award Examiners, Branches and Headquarters should be satisfied as to candidate's general competence to examine these awards. This special panel has been introduced in order to spread the work load and to meet the problem of examinations during school hours.

Grade 2 Examiners—Branch

(a)   Written application to Branch Secretary with two written references from Grade 1 Examiners.
(b)   Attendance at a minimum of three of a series of four lectures, as arranged by the Branch, at which the current Handbook and Examiners Manual will be required.
(c)   Attendance at an interview and oral examination by the Branch Examiners Panel.
(d)   Attendance at a practical test when the candidate Examiner will be required to examine a group (minimum 2, maximum 4) for the Bronze Medallion, in the presence of two specially appointed Grade 1 Examiners, who will submit a confidential report to the Branch Examiners Panel. (The Grade 1 Examiners will also adjudicate on the award candidates, clearing any points after the candidate Examiner has completed his examination of the group).
(e)   Appointment is subject to ratification by the Branch Executive.

On final appointment the candidate will receive a card of authority and Examiner's lapel badge.

Grade 2 Examiners—Headquarters

In non-branch areas in U.K. and overseas, the normal procedure will be as follows:

(a) Written application to Headquarters through the local Honorary Representative with two written references from Grade 1 Examiners and the Honorary Representative's comments.

(b) Headquarters arrange through the Honorary Representative the preparation of the candidate and the oral and practical tests. A confidential report on the tests will be forwarded to Headquarters.

(c) The successful candidate will receive a card of authority, Examiner's lapel badge.

(d) Modifications of the arrangements in (a) and (b) will be necessary in some areas.

Grade 1 Examiners

A Grade 2 Examiner may apply for appointment as a Grade 1 Examiner on completion of one year's service and a minimum of six separate life-saving examinations. If his application is accepted, he will be required to examine a group (minimum 2) for the Award of Merit or Distinction Award in the presence of two specially appointed Grade 1 Examiners, who will submit a confidential report to the Branch Examiners Panel or Headquarters as appropriate. (The Grade 1 Examiners will also adjudicate on the award candidates, clearing points after the candidate Examiner's examination is completed). Successful candidates will receive a new card of authority.

Renewal or Surrender of Card of Authority

Examiners' cards of authority are valid for one year and must show the date of expiry, by which date cards must be returned to the issuing authority for renewal, or surrender in the case of retirement (in the latter case the lapel badge should also be returned).

The National Executive reserves its own right and that of the Branch Executive Committees to refuse an application for appointment as a Grade 1 or Grade 2 Examiner without giving reasons for such refusal, and cannot engage in correspondence concerning such matters once a decision has been made. Similarly the right is reserved to remove an Examiner's name from the panel after giving due notice of such intention to the Examiner concerned at his last known address.

Moves

Examiners are earnestly requested to notify changes of address to Branches or Headquarters as appropriate. Examiners moving from non-branch to Branch (or vice versa) or to another Branch should notify both parties, enclosing their card for endorsement by the new Branch or Headquarters. Notification should be sent before the move and give the effective date.

THE LIFE GUARD CORPS

The trained life saver, like the trained first aider, is ready to use his individual skills when a sudden emergency occurs. A growing number of trained life savers go a step further in giving a voluntary service to the public at weekends. The Life Guard Corps, through its clubs, enables popular bathing places at the sea or inland to be watched by teams trained and equipped for rescue.

Here is a worthwhile job, which combines a service to the community with physical activity and companionship. Considerable progress has been made in the task of expanding the Life Guard Corps into the nucleus of a national service. A tremendous effort will be needed over the next few years to achieve the national coverage required.

Membership is obtained by joining a club. Details of the existing clubs (over 80 in 1969) can be obtained from Headquarters. These are the basic rules of membership:

(1)   Lifeguards may be men or women but must be members of Lifeguard Clubs recognised by the Society. They must hold the Bronze Medallion and be over 18, or hold the Award of Merit and be over 16.

(2) Cadets must hold the Bronze Medallion and may be from 14 to 18 years old.

(3) Associate members of Clubs may be those in training to become qualified members or those who help in administration.

Awards

There is a special Proficiency Award for Lifeguards which requires skill in handling rescue craft, reel and line, as well as team rescue work in open waters.

Uniform

Lifeguards wear the distinctive badge of the Corps and a fluorescent hat to enable them to be readily recognised in case of need. The Corps organises local competitions and a National Championship.

How You Can Join

You can get help and information on setting up a post, or on joining or forming a Club, from Headquarters.

STARTING A CLUB OR INSTRUCTIONAL GROUP

Leadership

A successful life-saving club needs a leader or leaders whose enthusiasm sets the tone. It is usually the leader who will initiate the formation of a club.

Premises and Water Time

Before considering starting a club there must be an assurance that the minimum facilities can be secured. These are:

(1) Water-training time, ideally in a heated swimming pool which can be used throughout the year: but a club can be sustained on the basis of water time in summer only, if an imaginative winter programme is organised.

This may mean:

   (a) the use of quieter public periods;
   (b) the use of normal club or school sessions;
   (c) special affiliation to Local Baths Authority for exclusive use for regular periods;
   (d) special terms of hire.

(2) A regular meeting place. Some clubs meet only at the baths but an effort should be made to find premises for lectures, meetings, social and fund-raising activities. Education authorities will often assist by hire or free loan of schools or other educational premises.

A meeting room or hall should have adequate furniture, satisfactory ventilation and be suitable for showing films and slides.

Equipment

Equipment is needed particularly for training in resuscitation and is generally expensive to purchase. If Life Guard patrols are undertaken more equipment will be required (over a period of time).

Consideration should be given to making or improvising equipment. There is great scope for inventiveness and "do-it-yourself".

Equipment for Resuscitation Training

A wide range of training aids are available at various prices. Many are advertised in the Journal. The most popular are:

The Cheshire Wilson Training Aid.
The Resusci-Anne range.
The Ambu range.

General Equipment

The following will prove useful for various aspects of training: mats, towels, blankets, blackboard, charts and boarding for their support, diving bricks, buoyancy aids.

Management and Organisation

Although in the first stages only one person may be at hand to start a club, he should be on the lookout for helpers, for the club can never succeed without a solid foundation of helpers.

A committee is desirable so that the work of running the club can be shared. A treasurer to collect subscriptions and take care of the finances and a secretary to deal with correspondence are necessary. There is some merit in appointing everyone to a specific job rather than electing general committee members — such posts might be badge secretary, subscriptions secretary, membership secretary, publicity officer, equipment manager. The younger members should also be considered for appointments, initially under supervision.

An important function of the Management Committee is to raise funds to support the club's work. Affiliation to local swimming associations and Youth Committees, etc. should be sought. Some authorities give grants towards the hiring of swimming baths and for equipment. Some give privileges to young people who gain the Bronze Medallion.

Finance

Regular income will be obtained from members' subscriptions and session fees but if these are the sole source of funds activities may be limited. Baths charges must be paid and equipment purchased. Donations should be sought and are often forthcoming in recognition of the public service nature of life-saving training.

Grant aid is normally available to any club affiliated to a Youth Committee and attention is drawn to the joint circular of the Ministry of Housing and Local Government (No. 40/67) and Welsh Office (No. 33/67).

It is wise practice to forecast the year's income and expenditure so that a definite target for fund raising can be set.

Recruitment and Publicity

It is difficult to offer specific advice on recruitment. In some areas almost all the eligible candidates may have to be recruited. In densely populated areas recruitment is apparently easier but there will be many counter attractions. Active recruitment and good publicity will be needed. Contact should be made with the local press and information supplied to them regularly on activities and awards. Recruitment information should be sent to schools in the area. The Physical Education Organisers of the Local Education Authority can give valuable advice. Local places such as public libraries will often display material. Display stands can be put on at many local events such as safety conferences, fetes, exhibitions, etc. A keen lookout should be kept for friendly amateur photographers so that pictures can be collected to illustrate displays. Branches or Headquarters can supply leaflets and posters.

Liaison

Essential liaison will be with Baths Committees and Baths Managers; the press; Education Authorities, in particular the Chief Education Officer and the Physical Education Organiser, the Society's local representative. Good liaison will bring in help of many kinds and new members.

Training

Training programmes will depend upon the standard of proficiency of the membership, but some general hints are possible. A reasonable balance must be kept between theory and practice, between resuscitation and water work (see Section VI, on "Hints to Teachers"). Above all, training must be progressive; each session including revision, practice and new work.

Clubs can give a particularly useful contribution to publicising the work of the Society by training demonstration teams.

Thought should be given to the formation of a Life Guard section, which could in time become a separate Life Guard Club, so that the training can be put to practical use.

Liaison with both beach and river Life Guard Clubs would enable members to get sea and river experience under skilled supervision.

Progressive Responsibility

The club with young people in its membership will succeed when it involves them in its activities to the extent that they feel they have a real part in its running. Adults are often reluctant to delegate responsibility but they must weigh the long-term advantages against some possible immediate failures. Every member should be looked at as a potential helper and instructor.

NOTES ON WATER SAFETY LECTURES

The Society has accepted responsibility for general instruction to the public in water safety, with particular reference to supervision of children and advice to those likely to spend holidays at the seaside, especially where surf conditions prevail (North Devon and Cornwall).

Short talks can be given to Rotary and Round Table meetings, Women's Institute meetings etc. A film "Water Safety", (running time 40 minutes) is available from Headquarters.

The following format might be used as a guide for those preparing water safety lectures:

General

The drowning problem — the facts and the dangers of "open water".

The causes of drowning accidents.

The circumstances of drowning accidents.

In general terms what needs to be done to combat these causes and circumstances.

Specific

The rules of water safety for young children, parents, non-swimmers; the bather: at the pool, at the beach, in the river or lake; the boater or canoeist; the fisherman etc.; the dangers of ice.

What to do if in difficulty.

How to help others ("reach–throw", etc., and resuscitation).

The dangers of swimming rescue and the need for training.

Special responsibilities of those in charge of groups of young persons in regard to water activities.

The training which the Society offers and how to obtain it.

The opportunities offered by the Life Guard Corps for service.

RESCUES

Rescue Reports

Reports of rescues should be forwarded to Headquarters on the proformas available from Headquarters, Branches, Life Guard clubs and Honorary Representatives. The proforma is reproduced on pages 134 and 135.

The information is valuable for assessing the value of techniques and also for consideration for the Mountbatten Medal.

Reports should also be phoned to the local press, mentioning the name of the Society.

Too few reports are being sent in at present.

Mountbatten Medal

The Mountbatten Medal is awarded annually by Admiral of the Fleet The Earl Mountbatten of Burma, Grand President of the Society, to the holder of one of the Society's proficiency awards who performs the rescue adjudged the best of the year. The first medal was awarded in 1951. The name of recipients of the Mountbatten Medal are inscribed on a panel in the entrance hall of the Society's Headquarters.

Members of the Society and others who hear of rescues of sufficient merit are earnestly requested to report the details to the Society. An application form for consideration for the award of the Mountbatten Medal may be obtained from Headquarters. Completed application forms made in the United Kingdom and Eire must reach the Headquarters within two months, and others within four months of the date of the rescue. But reports of rescues made in the last weeks of the year must reach the Headquarters by 15th February in the following year.

The Royal Life Saving Society is a teaching and examining body and does not grant awards, other than the Mountbatten Medal, for saving life from drowning.

THE ROYAL HUMANE SOCIETY grants such awards, and application for recognition should be made to

The Secretary,
Watergate House, York Buildings, Adelphi,
London, W.C.2.

RESCUE OR INCIDENT REPORT FORM

Date and time of incident	
Place where incident occurred	
Name/s of person/s assisted or rescued	
Full address (and home address if on holiday) of above	
Name and address of person making report	
Name/s and address of witness	

Give full details of rescue or incident overleaf.

IT IS IMPORTANT THAT A REPORT IS MADE OF ALL INCIDENTS EVEN IF THE RESCUER WAS NOT IN ANY REAL DANGER SO THAT ASSESSMENT CAN BE MADE OF THE EFFICIENCY OF TECHNIQUES.

Return to The Royal Life Saving Society, Desborough House, 14 Devonshire Street, London, W.1

Signed.....................................

Date.....................................

DETAILS OF RESCUE OR ASSISTANCE GIVEN

1. **Circumstance**
   Include details of location; type of water (still, river, sea) weather conditions; number of people present; etc.

2. **Action Taken**
   Include details of aids or equipment if used; methods of release and rescue or nature of assistance given; state of victim; resuscitation if applied; result of resuscitation; other services involved (police, ambulance, first aid etc.)

ANALYSIS OF DROWNING STATISTICS

In alternate years Headquarters makes an analysis of reports supplied by Chief Constables on the causes and circumstances in which people are drowned in the United Kingdom.

In 1967, six hundred and ninety-two reports were examined and the following tables bear out the need for the teaching of water safety, swimming and life saving, particularly to the young.

Table 1

Distribution of accidents amongst types of water

Homes	..	..	..	42		
Canals	..	..	..	57		
Lakes and large reservoirs				38		
Ponds and small reservoirs				39		
Sand, gravel clay pits		..		29		
Rivers and Streams		..		238		

Estuaries ..	..	..	24
Sea..	..	..	137
Swimming pools..		..	30
Docks	..	..	30
Sewage Installations		..	6
Others	..	..	22

Table 2

Basic causes of accidents

Bathing and paddling
Bathing	..	..	90
Air-beds, inner-tubes, etc.			4
Attempting to rescue another	..	..	14
Swimming across a river			6
Retrieving ball, etc.	..		5
Paddling	..	..	15

Fishing 22

Boats 132

Accidents in homes
Bath	..	..	21
Ornamental ponds		..	5
Water-butts, tanks, etc.			4

Home-made rafts .. 10

Children playing near home 171

Fall from cliffs.. .. 7

Cut off by tide .. 7

Ice 6

Vehicles 26

Table 3

Distribution of accidents involving children drowned while playing near home

	0–5 years	6–10 years	11–15 years
Sand and gravel pits	4	6	2
Canals	10	15	1
Rivers and streams	43	24	2
Ponds	10	9	1
Lakes, reservoirs	6	2	1
Sewerage, open drains ..	4	3	—
Sea	2	11	1
Miscellaneous (works, tanks, etc.)	10	2	2

PUBLICITY

Public Demonstrations

Public demonstrations are an excellent way of bringing the work of the Society to general notice and every opportunity should be taken for arranging them — swimming galas, rowing regattas and other aquatic events, and especially the opening of a swimming pool in a new area.

All demonstrations should illustrate the need for life-saving training and should be linked specifically with name of the Society. Prevention of accidents by general water safety education should be stressed and mention made of the Life Guard Corps. A reel-and-line demonstration adds interest.

Although the detail of each demonstration will differ depending upon the audience, they should be planned basically to answer the following questions:

WHY — a short incident illustrating how a drowning accident happens.

HOW — a brief example of the skills required and the methods involved by which the Society tackles the problem. — The incident can be re-enacted to show correct action.

WHEN and WHERE local instruction can be obtained.

A supply of leaflets should be available.

Demonstrations, to be most effective, should be *short, sharp, entertaining and informative, NOT instructional.*

Press

The local press should be given reports of rescues and the results of examinations. It is a good idea to persuade the local papers to give a regular small column to the Society's local affairs.

Films

The Society's film "To Match Your Courage" is a useful lead-in to a talk to a school, etc. on the work of the Society, and can be obtained from Headquarters or most Branches.

Publicity Material

A list of charts, leaflets, posters, etc. can be obtained from Headquarters.

THE COMPETITION TROPHIES

There are many "live" and "points" competitions at Branch, National and Commonwealth level. A competitions committee has been set up to frame rules for a national and a schools life-saving championships.

The rules and details of entry for the following competitions can be obtained on application to the Headquarters or Branches. The competition year is 1st January to 31st December.

Commonwealth Trophies

THE WILLIAM HENRY MEMORIAL CUP is awarded to the individual Branch of the Society which shows the greatest percentage increase in the points obtained during the competition year.

THE SYDNEY J. MONKS MEMORIAL TROPHY is awarded to the individual Branch of the Society which obtains the highest figure for the number of Bars to the Bronze Medallion gained during the competition year.

THE KING EDWARD VII CUP is awarded to the affiliated school, club or other organisation which shows the greatest percentage increase in the points gained in the competition year.

THE GENERAL EXCELLENCE CUP. The competition for the General Excellence Cup is open to naval, military and Air Force Service schools, colleges and training establishments, and to naval and mercantile training ships.

United Kingdom Branch Trophies

PRIMARY AND SECONDARY SCHOOLS NATIONAL SHIELD. Open to all schools giving full time education and affiliated to the Society.

For the School gaining the highest percentage of points for examination in the Society's Resuscitation Proficiency Awards.

THE DARNELL EXCELLENCE CUP. Open to Boys' Schools and Boys' sections of Mixed Schools, affiliated to the Society.

For the school which obtains the highest percentage from boys eligible for Bronze Medallion and Bar to Bronze Medallion awards.

THE MRS. HENRY CUP. Open to Girls' Schools and Girls' sections of Mixed Schools affiliated to the Society.

For the School which obtains the highest percentage from girls eligible for Bronze Medallion and Bar to Bronze Medallion awards.

JOHN V. HUDSON MEMORIAL TROPHY. Open to the following individual organisations (except Police Training Centres and Metropolitan Police Training Divisions) affiliated to the Society: schools providing full-time education, colleges, County, City and Borough Police Forces, Metropolitan Police Force (Divisions separately) and swimming clubs.

For the organisation which obtains the highest percentage from pupils or members eligible for Bronze Cross and Bar to Bronze Cross awards.

AFFILIATED CLUBS SILVER AND BRONZE CHALLENGE SHIELD. Open to all Ladies', Men's or Mixed Swimming Clubs affiliated to the Society.

For the Club showing the highest percentage of points gained in each year from the Bronze Medallion and higher awards.

SCHOOLS SAFETY AWARD CUP (formerly THE LADIES SILVER AND GILT CUP). Open to all schools giving full-time education affiliated to the Society.

For the school gaining the highest percentage of points for examination in the R.L.S.S. Safety Awards.

THE STUDENTS' SHIELD. For students in full-time attendance at Colleges of Further Education.

For the College showing greatest percentage of points gained in the calendar year from the Bronze Medallion and higher awards.

THEODORE SALVESEN MEMORIAL TROPHY. Open to pre-sea students of Nautical Colleges or Nautical Departments of established Colleges.

For the Nautical College or Nautical Department of an established College showing the greatest percentage of points gained in the calendar year from the Bronze Medallion and higher awards.

COLONEL WOODCOCK POLICE CUP. Open to County and Borough Police Forces of Great Britain and Northern Ireland (Police Forces of Greater London excepted).

Points may not be claimed for awards gained by members attending Police Training Schools or by Police Cadets.

For the Police Force obtaining the highest percentage of points in relation to the authorised strength of such Force, as published by the Home Office for that year (all life-saving awards to count).

THE BEATRICE STAYNES LIFE GUARD CORPS TROPHY. Open to Life Guard Corps Units.

For the Life Guard Corps Unit with the best percentage number of Life Guard Proficiency Awards and Bars gained in the competition year.

POLICE BATON — THE POLICE NATIONAL LIFE SAVING CHAMPIONSHIP.

ALINGTON CUP — THE POLICE (WOMEN) NATIONAL LIFE SAVING CHAMPIONSHIP.

WEST RIDING CUP — THE POLICE CADET (MEN) NATIONAL LIFE SAVING CHAMPIONSHIP.

ALINGTON CADET CUP — THE POLICE CADET (WOMEN) LIFE SAVING CHAMPIONSHIP.

THE OFFICIAL BADGES

The badge with the Royal Crown superimposed may be worn as a LAPEL badge by Officers of the Society (including appointed Examiners and Honorary Representatives) and as blazer and costume badges by holders of the Diploma and Distinction Awards. The badge with the Royal Crown superimposed MAY NOT otherwise be worn on uniform or other personal clothing.

Badges are manufactured in enamel as lapel badges and woven in silk on cloth for attachment to swimming costumes. The badges listed below can be purchased by holders of the appropriate awards.

Note: When ordering badges, the following particulars *must* be given and remittances should accompany order:

(1)   Name of class.

(2)   Awards held.

(3)   Year in which these were obtained.

The following badges may be purchased from Branches or Headquarters.

Costume Badges

Water Safety Award	3s. 0d.
Preliminary Safety	3s. 0d.
Advanced Safety	3s. 0d.
Preliminary Resuscitation	1s. 6d.
Advanced Resuscitation	1s. 6d.
Resuscitation Instructor	1s. 6d.
Bronze Medallion	4s. 6d.
Bronze Cross	4s. 6d.
Teacher	4s. 6d.
Life Guard Corps*	4s. 6d.
Cadet*	4s. 6d.
Proficiency	4s. 6d.

Coat (Enamel Lapel Pin) Badges

Intermediate	4s. 6d.
miniature	4s. 6d.
Bronze Medallion	4s. 6d.
miniature	4s. 6d.

* Give membership particulars.
All prices are subject to revision.

Bronze Cross	4s. 6d.
Award of Merit	4s. 6d.
Distinction	4s. 6d.
Diploma	6s. 6d.
Teacher	4s. 6d.
Life Guard Corps*	5s. 0d.
Proficiency	5s. 0d.

Uniform Badges (Woven)

Scouts and Guides (for holders of Intermediate and above)	1s. 0d.
School Uniform — Bronze Medallion	1s. 0d.

* Give membership particulars.
All prices are subject to revision.

MEMBERSHIP

Advantages of Membership of the Society

Affiliation of classes, schools and clubs entitles members of such organisations to take examinations for the Society's awards without payment of individual membership subscriptions.

The *Handbook* is supplied to members and affiliated clubs and organisations at a special reduced price for a dozen or more copies.

All life governors and life members are members of the Council of the United Kingdom National Branch and receive the Commonwealth Annual Report.

Terms of Individual Membership

A donation of £15 15s. constitutes a Life Governor.

A donation of £10 10s. constitutes a Life Member.

A yearly subscription of not less than 10s. 0d. constitutes an Individual Member, who receives the Quarterly Journal.

Membership fees may be paid to Branches or Headquarters.

Affiliation

Local Education Authorities, Clubs and Associations should apply for details to Branches or Headquarters.

The yearly fee for all Schools and Training Colleges wishing to affiliate separately, Classes, Lifeguard Corps Clubs, etc., is 10s., which includes the Quarterly Journal.

Fees cover 12 calendar months dating from the first payment.

Journal

Those who do not receive the Quarterly Journal through membership or affiliation as above may become subscribers at 5s. yearly (post free).

THE SOCIETY NEEDS YOUR SUPPORT

How can *you* help the Society in the United Kingdom to develop and expand its work?

As an Individual

You can give active help by joining a class and taking a proficiency test or as a parent by encouraging your children to join; then by becoming:

an instructor;

or an examiner;

or an organiser.

If you cannot give active help, then financial help can be given in the following ways, by:

ordinary annual membership;

life membership;

life governorship;

covenant;

legacy.

As a Headmaster or Teacher or Youth Leader

Enable life-saving classes to be formed at your school or club.

As a Member of a Local Authority

Encourage:

the provision of swimming pools;

the Education Department to support the Society;

the formation of Life Guard Clubs.

As a Baths Manager

Give facilities and active help.

As an Industrial Firm

Give help towards the administrative costs of expansion and the provision of equipment and publicity material.

As a member of the Press, B.B.C. and Independent Television

Assist in bringing the work of the Society to notice on the widest scale.

As a leader of the Community

Give moral and practical support:

by encouraging the Society's local workers;

by putting over the case for greater support;

by pressing for the provision of facilties.

Index